MIND-BENDING MYSTERIES AND THRILLERS FOR TEENS

MIND-BENDING MYSTERIES AND THRILLERS FOR TEENS

A Programming and Readers' Advisory Guide

AMY J. ALESSIO

An imprint of the American Library Association
Chicago | 2014

AMY J. ALESSIO is a teen librarian at the Schaumburg Township District Library in Illinois. She writes and edits fiction and nonfiction, including two books coauthored with Kim Patton: *A Year of Programs for Teens* (2007) and *A Year of Programs for Teens 2* (2011). Her reviews have appeared in *Booklist* and *Crimespree Magazine* and on Teenreads.com. She served two terms on the YALSA Board of Directors and was honored in 2013 with the first Illinois Library Association Young Adult Librarian of the Year Award. She is passionate about cookbooks; she presents programs about them and writes about recipes on her Vintage Cookbooks and Crafts blog and on www.amyalessio.com.

© 2014 by the American Library Association

Printed in the United States of America
18 17 16 15 14   5 4 3 2 1

Extensive effort has gone into ensuring the reliability of the information in this book; however, the publisher makes no warranty, express or implied, with respect to the material contained herein.

ISBNs: 978-0-8389-1204-1 (paper).

Library of Congress Cataloging-in-Publication Data
Alessio, Amy J.
  Mind-bending mysteries and thrillers for teens: a programming and readers' advisory guide /
  Amy J. Alessio.
    pages cm
  Includes bibliographical references and index.
  ISBN 978-0-8389-1204-1 (alk. paper)
  1. Young adults' libraries—Activity programs—United States. 2. Teenagers—Books and reading—United States. 3. Young adult literature—Bibliography. 4. Detective and mystery stories—Bibliography. 5. Readers' advisory services—United States. I. Title.
  Z718.5.A43 2014
  027.62'6—dc23

                                                                    2013044195

Book design in Minion Pro and Gotham Narrow by Alejandra Diaz.

♾ This paper meets the requirements of ANSI/NISO Z39.48–1992 (Permanence of Paper).

CONTENTS

INTRODUCTION

There are plenty of mysteries in teen lives, including physical and emotional changes, uncertainty about the future, feelings between people. This ambiguity is likely part of the appeal of mystery stories for this age group. In many cases, the ending of a teen mystery book provides expected conclusions after an entertaining escape from reality. There is a natural progression of plot and clues to the end. No such path is provided in life.

Mystery fans often find their genre in childhood and pursue it through adulthood, as long as they can find more titles to read. The types of mysteries for adults are varied, and many resources exist that sort those types into cozies, police procedurals, and other subjects relevant to adult life. This book celebrates the mystery genre for young adult readers, breaking the genre into thematic categories for easier readers' advisory for this age group. The book also goes beyond booklists to recommend ways to booktalk and display each subgroup. Other chapters describe a Mind-Bending Mystery Club, programs for teens, and book discussion and marketing ideas. Readers today can find book recommendations online, but there are still plenty who do not know where to start to find books like some they love. This volume was written by a lifelong lover of the genre with over sixteen years of teen programming and readers' advisory experience. Writing it was an enjoyable experience that will hopefully translate into connections with teen readers and library users everywhere.

HOW IS THE BOOK ORGANIZED?

The first half of this book describes subgroups within the mystery genre and includes annotations for titles readers may enjoy. For example, in the first section, "Realistic Mysteries," titles and annotations are grouped into the following topics: Undaunted Detectives; Accused Teens; Disappearing Family and Friends; Small-Town Sleuths; Humorous Inspectors, or What's So Funny about Crime?; and Sporty Sleuths. At the end of each section are two mysterious booktalking examples and an idea for covert marketing. Most of the listed titles, including series titles, were published within the past eight years, but some classic teen and adult mystery writers have been included. Titles were chosen for quality or to match categories that I have found to be popular with teen readers. Some titles may not seem like tradition-al mysteries or may end unsolved, but readers of other titles in that grouping may enjoy them as well. The first part of this book is not meant to be a comprehensive overview of all teen mysteries; rather, it serves as a guide to what teen mystery readers may be looking for in new authors, titles, or series. In that same spirit, I have recommended some adult titles or series that older teens may enjoy.

Each book annotation was written with the teen reader in mind and could be used on a book list to hand to patrons. Suggested grade levels are provided, and many titles are cross-referenced under other categories, with the full annotation under the main subject heading for that book. The plus sign indicates books that may appeal to readers beyond grade 12. Series titles are given after the title of the first book in the series. Keeping series current within publication time lines is challenging, so the title of the series is used for the master lists provided in the appendix. Graphic novels are included in the annotations and grouped in a separate list in the appendix. The subject sections include interviews with several popular mystery authors to further help library staff learn about teen mysteries and trends.

Over forty program ideas are included in the second part of this volume, from passive puzzle-type programs to a complete mystery dinner script. Step-by-step program instructions can be found in chapter 4, and activities for the Mind-Bending Mystery Club are summarized in chapter 5. This separation reflects the different styles of the two approaches, though listed suggestions for the club could be made into larger programs and vice versa, providing flexibility for libraries of all sizes and situations. Many of the events described in the second part of the book also include adaptations for online use.

PART I
MYSTERIOUS READS FOR TEENS

Chapter One

TEEN MYSTERY READERS

Although today's teens may laugh at Nancy's crime solving in dresses and lipstick, there is no doubt that the publication of mystery series by the Stratemeyer Syndicate impacted the genre for youth readers. Readers got to know the characters as friends throughout the different series and to expect the plot and resolution patterns. Because readers' own lives were changing so much, it was a comfort to know what to expect from these books. The dangers and villains gave the books the feel of an exciting escape as well. It may be that those books now appeal more to younger teens because they are too predictable. The older Bobbsey Twins or Hardy Boys books especially may have cultural references that are unknown to today's readers.

So what are today's teen mystery readers looking for? They are certainly looking for more diversity, and, sadly, this genre still has a long way to go in that area. Although there are more situations and types of families, racial diversity is rare. Teens may find themselves portrayed in the situations or might empathize with the characters' feelings more than they would identify with Nancy Drew and her car, but diversity remains an area for improvement.

Teens are also looking for cross-genre appeal. Many adult cozy mysteries have a set pattern: a romantic police interest, food or a hobby, a small town. This combination seems to resonate with a lot of readers. For teens, no such identifiable pattern emerges. Rather, combining elements of other genres with teens who solve their own situations seems to be a successful approach. The appeal of teens solving crimes themselves or mainly by themselves is understandable. Crossing genres may help readers find comfort and familiarity with favorite books. There has not been a tradition of long-running teen mystery series or easily recognized teen mystery authors in the same way there has been for children or adults. In many cases teens still go right from youth mysteries to Agatha Christie. In some cases staff may not know what books or authors to recommend because a subject heading search for *mysteries for teens* does not pull up a streamlined traditional list. Instead, it brings up titles across the spectrum of the subgroupings listed in this book, which appeal to different types of teen readers. Giving a teen a Regency mystery in the same list as a dystopian thriller would be as off-putting as giving an adult a list with Grisham, food cozies, and Koontz. Teen literature as a whole is evolving, and future teen readers will find more mysteries, but for now finding ones that cross other genres or that have elements of suspense amid favorite types of books will be the hook.

MYSTERIOUS FOUNDATIONS

Most series that adults think of as youth mysteries were created by the Stratemeyer Syndicate. Edward Stratemeyer saw the potential for series targeted toward youth and published the Rover Boys' first volume in 1899. That series eventually sold over five million copies. Other youth series were created in the early years of the group, including the Bobbsey Twins in 1904, and Stratemeyer was busy hiring ghostwriters to keep up with demand. He became the first book packager for children.

One writer, Mildred Augustine (Mildred A. Writ Benson), was hired to write a Ruth Fielding series title in 1926. She ended up writing twenty-three of the first thirty Nancy Drew books. Known for her independent spirit, Mildred infused the new series with an unconventional feel, and the books caught on quickly after the first three were released in 1930. Sisters Harriet Stratemeyer Adams and Edna Stratemeyer Squier took over the company after their father's death in 1930, and Harriet ended up writing much of the Nancy Drew series after Mildred stopped. Mildred's typewriter is now housed at the Smithsonian Institution. (For more information about the Nancy Drew books, go to www.nancydrewsleuth.com/history.html.)

Other series, such as the Hardy Boys, the Happy Hollisters, and Tom Swift Jr., became very popular as well. Writers were never to reveal their authorship on the series, and until the syndicate ran into legal difficulties in the 1970s regarding hardcover versus paperback publishing, the secret was well kept.

Originally libraries did not want to include these series because of their perceived very light quality. As times and views changed, however, gatekeepers of books for children realized the positive impact of these series on fostering a love of reading.

As the readership for titles from the Stratemeyer Syndicate grew, other publishers began producing their own series, including Trixie Belden and the Three Investigators. Trixie and her friends were crime-solving teenagers, complete with crushes and awkwardness. Their stories began appearing in the late 1940s. In the early 1960s, the Three Investigators series also featured awkward but smart teens. Over time, both series had several different authors.

SUSPENSE NOVELS FOR TEENS

Suspense writing for young adults was also gaining momentum. From Rosamund du Jardin's romantic reads in the 1940s and 1950s to Mary Stewart's masterful romantic suspense tales in the late 1950s and beyond, teens were finding themselves in books and expanding their love of suspense, born in the earlier series, in new directions. In the late 1960s, Lois Duncan began writing suspense for teens. Her thrillers still find fans, though titles such as *Game of Danger* (1962) and *Ransom* (1966) are now over forty years old.

Teens and tweens in the 1970s through the 1990s also found such notable authors as Willo Davis Roberts and Joan Lowery Nixon. Just as Mary Stewart's titles helped develop the romantic suspense genre, V. C. Andrews and Ann Rule found their own readers with gothic suspense and true crime, respectively. Teens are still enjoying these authors, who remain unique in the field.

Some authors are continuing to create new, popular subgenres in teen mysteries, sparking inspiration in other authors. In 1990 Caroline B. Cooney published *The Face on the Milk Carton,* the first of a five-part series. Janie Johnson, the teen featured in the tetralogy, not only was to solve a crime, she was part of the crime herself. That plot twist marked the beginning of yet another subgenre and has been echoed many times by many other authors. Cooney continues to offer new types of books with over seventy published titles. She received her first and second Edgar Award nominations for *Diamonds in the Shadow* (2008) and *If the Witness Lied* (2010).

Also in the 1990s Vivian Vande Velde wrote fantasy and historical fiction that often crossed with traditional mystery. *Never Trust a Dead Man* won one of several Edgar Awards for this talented and popular author. Although fantasy and intrigue have long been married in fiction as characters puzzle out keys to kingdoms, J. K. Rowling's addictive story arc of the awkward teen wizard who has to solve a mystery in each book helped make fantasy and paranormal suspense mainstream.

While Christopher Pike was attracting horror readers in flocks during this same period, Todd Strasser and Michael Cadnum were also becoming known among readers of thrillers. Both of these authors continue to garner Edgar Award nominations. Nancy Werlin advanced dark thrillers for teens in the 1990s and received a National Book Award nomination and an Edgar Award for *The Killer's Cousin.* Also during this period, Gail Giles reached reluctant readers with her life-and-death, page-turning reads.

MYSTERIOUS REWARDS AND TRENDS

The old perception of mysteries as light reading is still reflected in book awards. Few of the Newbery winners or Honor titles are traditional mysteries, though Zilpha Keatley Snyder's *Headless Cupid* and Ellen Raskin's *Westing Game* are standouts. Lois Duncan is the only winner of the Margaret A. Edwards Award, given by the Young Adult Library Services Association, whose focus is suspense.

Mystery Writers of America has sponsored the mystery genre's best-known awards, the Edgars, since 1954. A category for juvenile mysteries was created in 1961 and for young adult mysteries in 1989. Bouchercon, the largest annual national mystery conference, has hosted the Anthony Awards since 1986. Juvenile and young adult titles are combined in one category designated a "wild card," and an award is not offered each year. The National Book Award has recognized young adult mysteries in recent years with a nomination for Nancy Werlin and an award for Judy Blundell's *What I Saw and How I Lied* (2008). Mysteries such as Marcus Sedgwick's *Revolver* and A. S. King's *Please Ignore Vera Dietz* have received recognition as Honor books by the Young Adult Library Services Association's Michael L. Printz Award. And true crime titles have frequently been among the recent YALSA Nonfiction Award and Honor Award recipients. Despite these honors, teen mysteries have yet to receive the literary recognition that other genres such as historical fiction or fantasy have gained.

Many authors of popular series for adults are now writing versions for younger readers, featuring their sleuths in earlier years. Other authors are trying young adult subjects after a successful career writing for adults, and still others are making a career out of writing exclusively for teens. Some long-standing teen mystery series are emerging that are more spy- or thriller-based, such as Anthony Horowitz's Alex Rider series or James Patterson's Maximum Ride series. The teens in those books do not solve crimes in hidden RV trailers as the Three Investigators did, but travel and use cutting-edge technology like young James Bonds.

The categories described in this book and the authors and titles featured all highlight the exciting new directions available for teen fans of mysterious reads.

ADULT MYSTERY NOVELS FOR TEENS

It can be challenging when younger teens are ready to move on to titles from the adult section. Reading abilities may be much higher than maturity, and books with lots of sexual conduct may not be appropriate. Often staff members direct teens to classic authors such as Agatha Christie, Sir Arthur Conan Doyle, or Dorothy Sayers. Titles from these authors provide excellent reading, are familiar to many, have modern media representations, and often appear on required reading lists for college-bound teens. There is nothing wrong with recommending classics, and titles from those authors can serve as starting places for many teens ready to read adult mystery titles for pleasure. However, teens who enjoy paranormal mysteries, for example, may not enjoy those choices, and the right readers' advisory approach will identify subgenres that will appeal to a wide range of mystery lovers.

Other classic authors will be found by teens themselves. For example, teens who like spy stories may find Ian Fleming on their own, especially as the Bond movies continue to be made. Lists of spy titles, both fiction and nonfiction, will help teens find others. And P. D. James's Adam Dalgliesh series, with its forensic approach to clues and the Scotland Yard connection, has the feel of Doyle and Christie.

Thrillers and *New York Times* best sellers are often found and enjoyed by teens whether staff recommends them or not. But by discovering which elements of mystery a teen prefers through in-person or online readers' advisory, matches can more easily be found. Teens who enjoy Grisham may like his youth series or titles from Brad Meltzer or David Baldacci. Lee Child's Jack Reacher is edgy and mature, and older teens who want to read those stories could also be directed toward Sandra Brown's suspense titles (instead of her romance stories) or Laura Lippman's psychological thrillers.

Many teens enjoy Janet Evanovich's humorous romantic suspense. Again the mature content is present, and the series has no similar counterpart in teen titles. The publication of graphic novels by Janet Evanovich will further interest teens in her work. Other adult titles with humor and mystery elements that may appeal to teens include those in the Spellman series from Lisa Lutz or books by Carl Hiaasen.

Forensic Files and *CSI* television viewers may pick up Kathy Reichs's series for teens, then the series for adults. Jan Burke's Irene Kelly series may also appeal to these teens. Michael Crichton and Dean Koontz are extremely popular with teens, as they combine the genres of science fiction or fantasy/paranormal with suspense. Teens who enjoy James Patterson's Maximum Ride series may not necessarily jump to Alex Cross, but they may want to try his diverse offerings. As mentioned in the introduction, other adult title and series recommendations will be made within the subject categories in this guide.

HELPING TEENS FIND THE RIGHT MYSTERY: A MYSTERIOUS READERS' ADVISORY

With over twenty categories of mysteries featured in this volume, matching the right teen to the right books may seem challenging. Many teens will not approach adults to ask about reading choices or, worse, will be forced to read titles assigned by parents or teachers. So how can staff members help teens? Successful in-person approaches include friendly, knowledgeable staff members and handouts for teens to peruse. Virtual readers' advisory is another powerful tool.

TIPS FOR IN-PERSON READERS' ADVISORY

Handing a teen a list of mystery titles on a bookmark may not help. If a teen enjoyed Marcus Sedgwick's historical mystery *Revolver* and the list contains Kimberly Derting's romantic paranormal suspense novel *The Body Finder,* that teen may not find another book she likes—and will not return for more help. The readers' advisory interview is like a flowchart with all paths eventually leading to the right book or resource. When a teen approaches your desk and says, "I'm looking for a mystery," here are some questions you may want to ask to pinpoint tastes:

Do you enjoy reading mysteries?
- Here the teen may mention he has to read one for school. The best answer to any response is, "We have lots of good ones."

What types of books do you enjoy?
- Try to lead the teen through a few other popular genre stories, like those by Anthony Horowitz, or titles with historical or paranormal elements. Hearing such phrases as "real life" or "stories of teens today solving crimes" may lead you to suggest some realistic titles.

Do you prefer fiction or nonfiction? What formats do you prefer?
- Try to determine whether the teen prefers fiction, true crime, or graphic novel formats. If the book is for an assignment, ask if a specific type is required.
- Offer lists of a few different genres. If the teen is still uncertain or not talking, pull some examples from different series. Or let her browse descriptions and annotations.
- As always, encourage teens to let you know what they think of the books when they are done so you can further pinpoint titles they may like.

 TIPS FOR VIRTUAL READERS' ADVISORY

How many clicks will it take teens to find a book suggestion on the library web page? If it is more than three or four, it is not likely they will pursue the effort, especially when it is easier to use Amazon.com, Barnes and Noble, or the library catalog. Rotate featured lists of books to go with popular titles or movies right on the main screen. A list of links directly on the teen page of reading resources or lists of titles with descriptions is another way to catch attention.

Putting titles and list links on Twitter may catch more adults than teens, but it is another way to reach readers. If you have a Mind-Bending Mystery Club or a display of materials is available, take photos of these activities and post them. Teens should find something new and book- or media-related each time they return to the library sites.

Chapter Two

MYSTERY SUBGENRES

This chapter will help take the mystery out of readers' advisory for mystery readers. Suggested titles are grouped by subgenre to best match teens' reading interests, and booktalking and marketing ideas are included. Some of the subgenres in this chapter, such as humorous mysteries, cross other genres, such as paranormal, but the books listed are good read-alikes for others in the subgenre. For quick reference, books are listed by subgenre and by author at the end of this book.

REALISTIC MYSTERIES

Realistic mysteries can happen anywhere in present-day situations. Realistic mysteries feature a variety of characters, from a kid lawyer (Grisham's *Theodore Boone*) to a modern-day Dashiell Hammett in Sean Beaudoin's *You Killed Wesley Payne*. Some involve robberies, cheating on tests, and more violent crimes. Small towns continue to be a favorite setting for fictional crimes, and the sleuths are no less savvy than their suburban or city counterparts. The setting just adds another element to the intrigue in those stories. Readers who enjoy nonfiction and true crime may also enjoy these realistic mysteries.

Interview with CAROLINE B. COONEY

Caroline B. Cooney has written almost eighty books for teen readers since 1979 in multiple genres, including paranormal, horror, mance, and, of course, mystery. Her titles have appeared on n ple notable books lists and have received numerous readers' ch awards. Her Face on the Milk Carton series and suspense titles a perhaps her best-known works. She garnered a nomination for the Edgar Award in 2010 for *If the Witness Lied* and in 2008 for *Diamonds in the Shadow*.

Q: Where did you get the idea for the Face on the Milk Carton series?

A: *The Face on the Milk Carton* was a stand-alone book. Its background is worry—years of terrible worry endured by the birth parents of a kidnapped child. I ended the story without wrapping it up so that my reader would also go on worrying. I was surprised to find myself doing a second book. *Whatever Happened to Janie?* came from a sermon at the church where I was then organist, and that sermon is referred to in the book: Who is the real mother (bearing in mind the biblical story of King Solomon and the infant claimed by two women)? *Voice on the Radio* was even more of a surprise to me—it's based on my son's stint in Boston on his college radio station and on my (negative) outlook toward talk radio and television. The fourth book, *What Janie Found*, came from an idea my editor, Beverly Horowitz, had—the concept of finding a piece of paper that would change the lives of everybody in the story. So a quartet was never planned! But I'm so glad it happened. I love the Janie books as much as anybody!

Q: What kinds of reactions have you had from readers about that series?

A: I have had many many letters and e-mails about the Janie books. My favorites are from kids who dislike reading but got hooked on the first book and went on to read the others and thank me for opening the door to reading. Such letters have made my life worthwhile.

Q: *Diamonds in the Shadow* and *If the Witness Lied* are very different from the Janie series. How did you approach those books?

A: *Diamonds in the Shadow* came about because I did have a family of four African Muslims live with me for a month when they came to America as refugees. The family in my book is entirely fictional and also Christian, but I could never have written it, or even thought of it, had I not been a participant in resettling refugees. *If the Witness Lied* is not based on a real event, but rather on my horror at how the media can invade a family and even control their fate, just as a form of amusement for viewers.

Q: Will you revisit Janie?

A: I certainly never meant to write a fifth Janie book, having carried her story as far as it would go. Or so I thought. Readers tend to ask the same two questions—do Janie and Reeve get married? Does the kidnapper get caught? But my editor, Beverly Horowitz, asked me to write an e-short story in which Janie and Reeve would be older—in college or out of it. This e-story (soon to come out as *What Janie Saw*) led to an entire book, because I too needed to know if Janie and Reeve got married and if the kidnapper got caught.

Interview with PATRICK JONES

Award-winning teen librarian and nonfiction author Patrick Jones came to fiction writing recently. His gritty, realistic titles deal with the mysteries of human behavior rather than traditional suspense, but his title *Cheated* led readers into psychological suspense based on a real event. His work and Cooney's are both examples of how teens who like a genre such as mystery may like different forms of realistic fiction as well.

Q: Although your books are described more as gritty, realistic stories, *Cheated* also reads like a thriller, in a style similar to *The Interrogation of Gabriel James*. In *Cheated*, Mick is going back over the story of how he got to the desperate place he is in, having committed a terrible crime with his two friends. Is *Cheated* based on anything in reality?

A: *Cheated* was, as they say, ripped from the headlines. This actual event—a group of teenagers who kill a homeless man because he cheated them out of money they gave him to buy beer—occurred near my hometown of Flint, Michigan. I was home visiting Flint and read the story in the paper, I think in the late 1990s, and I tucked it away. At this time I wasn't writing fiction, but still thought it would make an interesting story. As I was working on my first novel, *Things Change*, I remembered this incident and started to write. The first line was "Hey, Nail, where can we get some beer." But the book morphed into *Nailed*. At one time, the story of the bullied kid in *Nailed* was going to be the first part of the novel, and then when the mc [main character] went to a new school, he'd fall in with some rough kids as a way of protecting himself, which would lead to the murder. But I couldn't write it because I couldn't figure out a good ending. In the real case, one kid turned on his friends, but that is not a story I wanted to tell. So, the novel was inspired by a real-life event, but most everything else was made up. What is very odd is years later, I met at a school visit a teacher who had taught the kids, and it turns out my made-up backstories—failed athlete, imprisoned father, and broken kid from a broken home—did parallel [the lives of] the real kids involved. The other main difference I learned was the real murder was done in two parts and quite vicious, even involving torture, and I didn't want to go there. There was also a girl involved, but I wanted this to be a story only about fatherless sons and have no real romance element involved. The book *Cheated* most reminds me of is *Paranoid Park* by Blake Nelson, although *Cheated* shares almost the exact same cover as *Right Behind You* by the great Gail Giles, which, ironically enough, I blurbed.

Q: Did you know how Mick and his friends would get to that point of violence when you wrote the novel?

A: Yes, but I needed to know why. When I was writing the book and talking at school visits about how hard it was to figure out why these kids did this, some girl said the answer was easy: because they were drunk. Look, if every time a teenager got drunk [he or she] killed a homeless person, we'd have no homeless people. You could "cure that problem" just [on] a prom night. No, I needed both motive and opportunity even if the crime was not preplanned. I needed to show the anger, frustration, and rage bottled up [in] all three kids that causes two of them to snap and commit the crime. There is lots of violence foreshadowing the crime itself— everything about Brody is very violent, very physical, while with Mick, the main foreshadowing is with fire, which is his part of the crime. With Aaron, I wanted him to seem the less violent, very much the silent, ticking time bomb. Both Brody and Aaron grew up in violent homes; it is what they know.

Q: Do you read adult or teen mysteries? What are some you have enjoyed?
A: I read absolutely no adult fiction whatsoever and haven't for maybe twenty years. With teen books, I was a huge fan of Christopher Pike and R. L. Stine, even writing a whole book about R. L. Stine (*What's So Scary about R. L. Stine?*). Now, you could argue those are not mysteries, but thrillers or suspense with supernatural overtones. The same could be said of their forerunners whom I used to read and enjoy, like Lois Duncan and Joan Nixon. I do watch crime shows on TV, with a fondness for *Criminal Minds*, and I read nonfiction crime stuff, such as *Popular Crime* by Bill James. In high school, I recall very vividly reading *In Cold Blood*, *Helter Skelter*, and *Boston Strangler*, and faithfully "watching the detectives" like *Rockford Files* and *Columbo*. I really like Gail Giles, Nancy Werlin, and similar suspense writers.

Q: Did you intend to make *Cheated* a mystery, leading with clues and hints about the boys' pasts (both recent and long past)? How did your writing process differ with this title?
A: Part of my process has always been involving teens by finding a group to read a book in manuscript and then tell me what they think. It was directly as a result of this process that the structure of this book changed. My first version was three parts—the day of the murder, the day they got caught, and the interrogation—but the teens told me this [was] boring. They didn't have the patience for the foreshadowing and character development necessary so when the murder happens, it doesn't come as a total shock and you care about the characters and maybe, just maybe, want them to get away with it. So I instead used the classic device of letting you know on page one there was a murder, the main character is involved, and the mystery becomes not who did it, but why and even how. So to build the characters, I used a lot of both foreshadowing and backstory by telling of incidents in the past, since one of the themes is about how our past choices follow us forever. The mystery is why these kids on this night did this terrible thing, and when it happens, after you get over the shock, you should not be surprised if you've been paying attention. Then the second part of the mystery, of course, is will they get away with it and/or will one of them turn on the others.

Q: You have provided teen services and visits to detention centers. Do you think that helped you create the dimensional portrayals of the three boys that the book featured?

A: In a second draft, the "scenes" between the chapters were all set in JDC [juvenile detention center] and [had] Mick interacting with other kids. Another draft had him talking with police, and another with a counselor, but none of those worked. Instead, I realized that kids in detention have lots of free time to think, worry, and backtrack their lives. *How did I get here?* The other way that work informed the book is simple: often people will talk about a kid landing behind bars because of a "bad choice," and I hate that. It is rarely *one* bad choice; instead, it is a series of choices often made years in the past that lead to a criminal act. It is nature and nurture; it is opportunity and enabling. And it's not easy: that's why I start the book with two conflicting quotes about choices and regrets. The three boys also represent the three kids I meet most often in corrections: the Aarons, the kids who are criminals/sociopaths and nothing is going to change them; the Brodys, the kids who grow up around violence and have nothing positive in their lives, and so they turn to violence, not as a choice, but as a natural reaction; and finally the Micks, the kids who get in with the wrong people at the wrong time for the wrong reasons and bad stuff happens. Some of the lines in the book, like when Mick's lawyer says something like, "There's what's right, what's wrong, and what they can prove," are things I overheard directly from kids at JDC.

Q: Has the reaction to *Cheated* differed from reactions to other books you have written?

A: Well, I don't get anywhere [close to] the response I do from my other books, other than questions about "what happens next?" Looking back, I can't say I'm surprised. These are very angry kids, and it's hard to be around them. But when I do school visits, *Cheated* causes a lot of discussion and debate about what Mick should have done differently. Half of the kids think he should have ratted on his friends, the other half think he should stay loyal. Most of the questions are from girls about Cell Phone Girl, who in an early version had a much bigger role in the story.

Q: Do you have stories of other crimes or mysteries that you would like to write?

A: I have two books I've yet to publish which certainly have crime/mystery elements, but again, not pure mystery. In *Clicked*, you learn in the first chapter that the main character's sister ran away on Christmas morning three years ago, but you don't know why, and most of the book is him searching for that answer. The incident is foreshadowed in that first chapter (a gun allusion) and partially revealed about halfway through. The main character only heard what happened, but didn't see it. It is not until the end of the book that the sister reveals what she did with the gun. The other novel is called *Control Group: A Fair and Balanced Novel*. It starts with two characters (Clinton and Latasha) showing up at the door of a third (Rosie). Rosie asks what they want, and Latasha says, "We're here to kill you." Then the story cuts back to nine months before. There's a pretty high body count in this one, and the mystery of who is killing these kids is solved by Clinton and his friends, not by the police. But I'd say the mystery element is only one part of it. It is also about race, religion, and politics. In other words, the three things you're never supposed to deal with directly in a teen novel. It's like nothing else out there, including a subplot about a charismatic, conservative, and ambitious female politician (Tara Fallon) who has a daughter (Crystal Fallon) who gets pregnant when her mom is running for higher office. Crystal does not, however, appear on a television dancing program. I think it's a unique book, albeit for a small audience, and if I can't find a publisher I might go the self-publishing route because I think it's an important book with political rather than personal issues that teens should be thinking about in our teach-to-the-test/increase-scores-at-all-costs culture.

❱ UNDAUNTED DETECTIVES

Carter, Ally. *Heist Society* (Heist Society series). Hyperion, 2010.
>Katarina Bishop tries to separate from her art-thieving family by going to boarding school, only to get kicked out. In the first title of this fun series, she has to save her father, who has been falsely accused of stealing five paintings from a dangerous man. How can she save him? By stealing them back. (Gr. 6+)

Cortez. Sarah. *You Don't Have a Clue: Latino Mystery Stories for Teens.* Piñata Books for Young Readers, 2011.
>This collection of ten stories introduces readers to some of today's best Latino writers as teen characters solve crimes from kidnapping to murder. (Gr 7+)

Fredericks, Mariah. *Crunch Time*. Atheneum Books for Young Readers, 2007.
>Nominated for the 2007 Edgar Award, this subtle psychological mystery features four teens studying for the SAT at a prep school. They learn that someone among them has paid another person to take the test, and the story explores everyone's motivations. (Gr. 8–11)

Grisham, John. *Theodore Boone: Kid Lawyer* (Theodore Boone series). Puffin, 2011.
>Younger teens will enjoy the smart stories of 13-year-old Theo, whose parents are lawyers in a small town. He himself is something of a lawyer who helps underdogs and fights crime. This title won the 2010 Agatha Award. (Gr. 5–9)

McClintock, Norah. *Dooley Takes the Fall* (Ryan Dooley Mysteries). Red Deer Press, 2008.
>McClintock is a master of the short, suspenseful tale, making these books great choices for reluctant readers. Ryan, fresh out of juvenile detention, and

his ex-cop uncle find themselves fighting for justice and solving murders. Rough but sympathetic, these characters will appeal to older teen boys. (Gr. 9–11)

McGowan, Anthony. *The Knife That Killed Me.* **Delacorte, 2010.**
Paul is bullied into delivering a package and becomes entangled with gang warfare at his school. He begins to find allies, but at the same time has to learn what his boundaries are after he realizes that holding a knife makes him feel powerful. A great book for discussion for older teens. (Gr. 9+)

Neri, G., and Randy DuBurke. *Yummy: The Last Days of a Southside Shorty.* **Lee and Low, 2010.**
Based on the 1994 murder of a 14-year-old girl by an 11-year-old boy during a gang shooting on Chicago's South Side, this graphic novel takes readers into the background of the painful story. As the story of Robert "Yummy" Sandifer unfolds, questions are raised about whether he actually killed anyone and how the gang was involved. (Gr. 8+)

Reid, Kimberly. *My Own Worst Frenemy* **(Langdon Prep series). Dafina, 2011.**
Chanti moves from a public school to a wealthy, private Denver school on scholarship after her vice cop mom worries for her safety in their neighborhood. It is clear that the headmistress and some of the privileged girls want her to leave. She and her crush, Marco, have to defend themselves when they are accused of thefts, though Chanti hopes her secretive new best friend, Bethanie, isn't the real criminal. Diversity and humorous commentary on class make this series a breath of fresh air in the mystery world. (Gr. 8+)

Renn, Diana. *Tokyo Heist.* **Viking, 2012.**
Manga-loving Violet thinks her dreams have come true when she has to go with her father to Japan. But soon she is involved in solving an international art crime as she tracks down clues so her father will not be in danger. Details of Japanese culture and life richly enhance the modern setting. Violet works on her own manga story while taking part in an exciting caper in this well-crafted tale. (Gr. 7–10) For discussion suggestions, see chapter 6, "When Book Discussions Get Mysterious."

Shoemaker, Tim. *Code of Silence* **(Code of Silence series). Zondervan, 2012.**
What should you do if you witness a violent robbery? Three suburban Chicago friends find themselves in danger as they struggle with choices after seeing the crime. When an innocent man is accused, they reach for justice even when it puts them in peril. An interesting story for younger teens to read and discuss. (Gr. 5–8)

Stratton, Allan. *Borderline*. HarperCollins, 2010.
Sami is embarrassed by his father, who is always pulling him away from hoops with friends Marty and Andy for prayers. His father also put him in a private school after a girl accused him of being perverted. When his father cancels a planned weekend for the two of them and instead goes on his own, Sami goes to his friends' cabin without their parents. His father is furious, but seems to be keeping secrets of his own. When the FBI accuses his father of terrorism, Sami retraces his father's last trip to clear his name. (Gr. 9+)

ADULT REALISTIC MYSTERIES FOR OLDER TEENS

Barr, Nevada. *Track of the Cat* (Anna Pigeon series). Putnam, 1993.
In this unique series set in our national parks, smart and clever park ranger Anna uses her skills at finding clues in nature to solve the mysteries. This unusual approach will appeal to high school–age readers. (Gr 9+)

Ferraris, Zoe. *Finding Nouf* (A Katya Hijazi and Nayir al-Sharqi Novel). Houghton Mifflin, 2008.
In the first title of this contemporary Saudi Arabian series, the body of a teenage girl is found, and desert guide Nayir al-Sharqi determines to find out what happened. Katya Hijazi, a forensic worker in the coroner's office, defies convention with her uncovered head and independence, but becomes an ally of Nayir. (Gr. 9+)

Lupton, Rosamund. *Sister: A Novel*. Broadway, 2011.
When her sister Tess's death is labeled a suicide, Beatrice becomes determined to prove that it was murder, although many of Tess's own choices led to the event. The love between the sisters makes this an emotional thriller that will connect with teens. (Gr. 9+)

▶ ACCUSED TEENS

When teens have to clear their name or that of someone close to them, the result is exciting reading. Sometimes the teen is guilty of the crime, which also makes for an intriguing read.

Fusili, Jim. *Marley Z and the Bloodstained Violin*. Dutton, 2008.
When Marley's friend Marisol is accused of stealing a $500,000 violin from Juilliard during a class trip, Marley jumps in to prove her innocence. A security videotape shows Marisol taking the violin, but she has no memory of doing so. Marley's search for answers is woven among interesting and realistic scenarios with family and friends. This mystery for younger teens features New York City as a strong and enjoyable presence. Music underlies the narrative, which is not surprising, as Fusili writes adult music nonfiction books as well. (Gr. 5–7)

Godwin, Jane. *Falling from Grace.* **Holiday House, 2007.**
When 12-year-old sisters Annie and Grace climb a rock during a storm on an Australian beach, Grace disappears. Fourteen-year-old Kip finds the girl's backpack. Former beach-shack musician Ted gives Kip a rum-laced Coke, and police become suspicious of both of them. The story alternates between Annie's and Kip's points of view as the search for the missing girl heightens. (Gr. 8–10)

Henderson, Lauren. *Kiss Me Kill Me* **(Scarlett Wakefield series). Delacorte, 2008.**
After a boy dies during their first kiss, Scarlett transfers to the school her family runs, Wakefield Hall, ready to put the tragedy behind her. But someone knows that there is more to the incident than an allergic reaction gone horribly wrong. An anonymous note inspires Scarlett to find out what really happened in this British mystery. (Gr. 8–12) For discussion suggestions, see chapter 6, "When Book Discussions Get Mysterious."

Jones, Patrick. *Cheated.* **Walker, 2008.**
Growing up in Flint, Michigan, has set Mick Salisbury on a path to making some wrong choices. But sitting in a police interrogation room, he realizes that the night things came to a crisis for him and his friends has led him to a crossroads, and he now has to make the most important choice of his life. Based on a true story, this suspense novel for older readers is great for discussion. (Gr. 9+)

Ludwig, Elisa. *Pretty Crooked* **(Pretty Crooked Trilogy). HarperCollins, 2012.**
Her mother's success in business means Willa gets to go to a pricey new private school and buy whatever she wants with credit cards. Her new designer duds make her part of the Glitterati, or popular girls. But a mean-girl blog picks at the scholarship girls, and Willa feels sorry for them. She steals from the Glitterati and buys designer duds for the victims of the bullying. She is also drawn to Aidan, another student with secrets. When she is caught, she learns who she can trust in this first of a new series. (Gr. 8+) *See also* Romantic Suspense.

Runholt, Susan. *The Mystery of the Third Lucretia* **(Kari + Lucas Mystery series). Puffin, 2009.**
Kari and Lucas are treated harshly by a man copying a painting in Minneapolis. When they travel to London, they see the same man at another museum and soon find themselves investigating an international art forgery case. Friendship, travel, and art make this unique and well-written series enjoyable reading for younger teens. (Gr. 6+)

Schrefer, Eliot. *The Deadly Sister*. Scholastic, 2010.
> When Abby looks at the body of Jefferson Andrews, she knows she is going to have to cover for her sister Maya—again. She's been doing that their entire lives, and now Maya's boyfriend has been murdered. Abby takes action to protect her sister and to find out what really happened in this twisting psychological suspense story for older teen readers. (Gr. 9+)

▶ DISAPPEARING FAMILY AND FRIENDS

Nothing fires the imagination like a missing persons case. Sometimes people want to leave, and those left behind have to struggle to understand the motive. At other times, those who vanish have no choice. These titles are especially powerful for teens as they are preparing to let go of family and childhood and become adults.

Abrahams, Peter. *Reality Check*. HarperTeen, 2010. (Gr. 8–11)
> See Thrillers–Thrilling Reading.

Bradbury, Jennifer. *Shift*. Atheneum, 2008.
> Chris is beginning his first semester in college when FBI agents knock on his door. Chris and his best friend, Win, spent the entire summer riding their bikes across the United States, but only Chris came home. Now the FBI is looking for Win. As Chris thinks back over the summer and their conversations, he realizes he may indeed know what happened to his friend. (Gr. 9+) *See also* Realistic Mysteries—Sporty Sleuths.

Brooks, Kevin. *Black Rabbit Summer*. Chicken House (Scholastic), 2008.
> A get-together with former high school friends turns deadly in this psychological thriller for older teen readers. Pete is pulled in when his ex-girlfriend asks him to come to the party and drags along unpopular loner Raymond. Before the end of the night, a girl is dead, and Raymond is a suspect. Pete looks hard at the others who were there that evening, including Nicole's twin brother, Eric, and uneven Pauly—even as police consider Pete a suspect. Brooks weaves layers and surprises into this story of why growing up and letting go are impossible for some people. (Gr. 10–12)

Burak, Kathryn. *Emily's Dress and Other Missing Things*. Roaring Brook Press, 2012.
> Claire's best friend Richy has disappeared, and she was the last person to talk to him. She lives in the town of Amherst, and when Emily Dickinson's dress disappears from a museum, Claire knows it is in her closet. She brings student teacher and friend Tate on a trip to find Richy—and themselves. (Gr. 8+)

Cooney, Caroline B. *If the Witness Lied*. **Delacorte, 2009.**

Nominated for a 2010 Edgar Award, this story follows Jack as he is left to care for his 3-year-old brother, Tristan, after the death of their parents. Jack's sisters find other places to live, and only his step-aunt is left, a guardian in name only. Tristan indirectly caused his mother's death (she had cancer while carrying him), and he supposedly killed his father as well by releasing the brake and allowing the car to roll over the man. Now Jack's aunt wants the family, and especially the little boy, to appear on TV on the anniversary of the father's death, lured by a lucrative media deal. Jack and his sisters close ranks to protect Tristan. As they come together, they begin to question what they have been led to believe. Things unfold quickly as they fight to stay together. (Gr. 8–10)

Gerber, Linda. *The Death by Bikini Mysteries* (*The Death by . . . Mysteries series*). **Speak (Penguin), 2011.**

Aphra Connolly loves her island life, helping her dad run their hotel. But her mother's disappearance four years ago continues to trouble her, especially when she learns mysterious guests at the hotel may know something about it. The titles in this series have been brought together into a new, single volume, and readers will enjoy having all the adventures together. (Gr. 7–10) *See also* Romantic Suspense.

Green, John. *Paper Towns*. **Dutton, 2008.**

Winner of the 2009 Edgar Award, this story follows Quentin as he tries to discover what happened to missing neighbor Margot after they spent an exciting night taking revenge on people in her past. Margot left him clues, but the more he learns about Margot, the less he seems to know. (Gr. 8–12)

Henry, April. *Girl, Stolen*. **Henry Holt, 2010.**

While her mother gets a prescription filled, blind teenager Cheyenne falls asleep in the car, only to awake and discover she has been kidnapped by a car thief. When the young man learns her father is the president of Nike, his hard-core criminal family develops worse plans for Cheyenne. The two teens cautiously learn to trust each other and to find a way out of the escalating situation. (Gr. 8–11)

Henry, April. *The Night She Disappeared*. **Henry Holt, 2012.**

Gabie drives a Mini Cooper. When coworker Kayla goes missing, Gabie learns that a customer, the possible kidnapper, asked if the girl with the Mini Cooper was working. Gabie thinks she was supposed to be the victim and becomes obsessed with finding Kayla, tracing her steps in an effort to save her. The point of view of a killer who is obsessed with Gabie is interspersed with the thoughts of all involved in this nail-biter. (Gr. 8–11) *See also* Romantic Suspense.

Northrup, Michael. *Gentlemen.* **Scholastic, 2009.**
Mike worries a bit when his friend Tommy, who usually answers his cell phone, stops communicating. Mike and his friends from remedial classes, Mixer and Bones, assume Tommy will be back soon. Then their English teacher asks them to put a mysterious barrel in the trunk of his car. The more the boys talk, the more they are convinced the teacher has killed Tommy. Then Mike catches Bones date-raping a girl from their classes, a girl Tommy had a crush on. He isn't sure who to trust now, but the three boys nonetheless decide to take action—for Bones, however, action means weapons, and the situation is soon out of control. Mike is frozen and becomes a witness to a terrible scene between Bones and the English teacher. Although the ending leaves some hope, this realistic, edgy title for older teens will haunt readers. (Gr. 10–12)

Plum-Ucci, Carol. *Following Christopher Creed.* **Harcourt, 2011.**
This sequel to *The Body of Christopher Creed* (2000), a Michael L. Printz Honor Award title, seeks to find the answers left at the end of the first selection. College reporter Mike has been following the case of Chris Creed. When a body is discovered in Steepleton, Mike thinks this is his big break. He finds the broken family of Chris Creed and becomes involved with them. Plum-Ucci is the master of the surprise twist, and this book is no exception. (Gr. 9+)

Shepard, Sara. *The Lying Game* **(Lying Game series) HarperTeen, 2011; and**
Pretty Little Liars **(Pretty Little Liars series) HarperTeen, 2006.**
Both of these popular TV tie-in series involve missing people. In *Pretty Little Liars*, four high school juniors try to learn what happened to their friend who disappeared three years ago. They are being threatened and receive notes and texts from mysterious people. In *The Lying Game*, a teen girl disappears, and a previously unknown twin sister steps into her place to find out who killed her. (Gr. 8–11)

Taylor, Brooke. *Undone.* **Walker, 2008.**
Shy Serena is a self-proclaimed geek in a small town, until Kori chooses to be her friend in eighth grade. Serena's mother, however, believes Kori is a bad influence and does not want the girls to spend time together. When Kori is killed in a car crash, Serena finds a list of things her friend wanted to do. Some things on the list make no sense, such as "making things right with Shay." To honor Kori, Serena tries to find Shay and help make things right, but soon finds she is involved in Kori's secrets—more than she ever imagined. (Gr. 8–11)

Valentine, Jenny. *Me, the Missing and the Dead.* **HarperTeen, 2008.**

A finalist for the 2009 YALSA William C. Morris YA Debut Award, this unusual mystery begins with an urn left in a taxi. Sixteen-year-old Lucas sees the urn and feels sorry for whoever left it. It almost seems to be reaching out to him. He brings the urn home and begins to research Violet Parks, the name engraved on it. Violet ends up being connected to Lucas, and the search even provides him with some clues about his missing father. Excellent psychological mystery for older teens. (Gr. 9+)

Weingarten, Lynn. *Wherever Nina Lies.* **Point (Scholastic), 2009.**

Ellie is still haunted by the disappearance of her sister, Nina, two years ago. After finding a clue in a thrift shop, Ellie locates a party house where Nina may have gone before she vanished. Ellie finds some threads of Nina's story and learns about a possible location to try in Nebraska. Then she meets Sean, who offers to take her to Nebraska. Ellie is attracted to him and agrees to go even though she just met him. Readers will know before Ellie does that there is something sinister about Sean, and although the story has a good ending, it is definitely a page-turner for older teens. (Gr. 11–12)

❱ SMALL-TOWN SLEUTHS

Always popular with adult readers, small-town sleuths are now making their way into the teen readership. The theme of wanting to grow up and get out is prevalent, though many teens find it hard to let go entirely when they get caught up in a crime.

Abrahams, Peter. *Down the Rabbit Hole* **(Echo Falls Mystery series). Harper-Collins, 2006.**

Ingrid Levin-Hill simply wants to play soccer and act on stage. But instead she finds herself stubbornly trying to find out what happened when some people in her town are killed. Sometimes she discovers things she would rather not know about other people in her small town—even about her own family members. (Gr. 5–8) *See also* Realistic Mysteries—Sporty Sleuths.

Beaufrand, Mary Jane. *The River.* **Little, Brown, 2010.**

Veronica hates her family's new small town in rural Oregon in this 2011 Edgar Award–nominated title. Sunny little Karen, a neighbor's child, cracks her defenses. When Veronica finds Karen's body in the river, she determines to find out what happened. Her grief not only blinds her to a friend's serious problem but also clouds her judgment about the boy she likes as she heads into danger in this page-turner. (Gr. 7–9)

Ford, John C. *The Morgue and Me*. Viking, 2009.

Nominated for an Edgar Award in 2010, this well-crafted mystery follows accidental detective Christopher. The sleuth finds a bag of money in his supervisor's office during his work at the morgue and knows it is connected to the body that just came in. No way should the death be labeled a suicide when the body has five bullet holes in it! Chris takes pictures of the body and then begins to investigate, which is not easy in his small town. It becomes even more difficult when he realizes that everyone around him seems to be connected to the cover-up, including his best friend. The pace gains speed until the harrowing conclusion, in which Chris is forced to shoot someone to save himself. This take on the classic detective story is realistic and edgy enough for older teens. Ford is definitely an author to watch in the mystery genre. (Gr. 10–12) *See also* High-Tech Whodunits—CSI Teens.

Hautman, Pete, and Mary Logue. *Snatched*. (Bloodwater series). Putnam Juvenile, 2006.

Eleventh-grade reporter Roni meets freshman scientist Brian, and the unlikely pair delve into kidnapping and worse in their small town. Although they don't always get along, they are believable and engaging characters as the suspense rapidly propels this series for younger teens. (Gr. 5–8)

Mackall, Dandi Daley. *The Silence of Murder*. Knopf, 2011.

In this 2012 Edgar Award winner, 16-year-old Hope Long tries to defend her brother, Jeremy, when he is accused of killing his beloved baseball coach. Jeremy has not spoken since he was little, and their mother, who has been mostly a negative presence in their lives, wants him declared insane. Hope knows her brother didn't commit murder, but as she tries to discover what did happen, she learns that she cannot trust people in her small town. Readers will realize with Hope that Jeremy has been trying to communicate all along in this well-crafted adventure. (Gr. 8–10)

Parker, Robert. *The Boxer and the Spy*. Philomel, 2008.

This stand-alone title features 15-year-old Terry Novak, who, in the midst of boxing training and wooing smart girl Abby, uncovers a network of small-town lies. When the body of classmate Jason washes up on shore, Terry and Abby do not believe it was a suicide. When they begin asking questions, they are threatened by everyone from the town bully to the principal of their school. Terry and Abby's flirting provides some fun interplay in this dark tale, and readers will be very interested in the boxing training when they realize Terry will have to call upon it soon. (Gr. 7–9) *See also* Realistic Mysteries—Sporty Sleuths.

Pfeffer, Susan Beth. *Blood Wounds.* **Harcourt Children's Books, 2011.**
Willa does not know she has a father until she learns she is in danger. Budge, her birth father, is on the run after killing three sisters Willa did not know she had, and many think he is coming to hurt Willa and her mother. Willa insists on going to Texas for the funerals, where she learns about years of secrets her mother has kept. Finding out who she is helps her figure out who she wants to become. (Gr. 8–10)

Reiss, Kathryn. *Blackthorn Winter.* **Harcourt, 2006.**
Juliana and her siblings have to move to rainy England when their parents separate. The new location forces into her mind disturbing pieces of her forgotten first five years. When her mother's best friend and neighbor is murdered and evidence is found in their house, Juliana knows she must find out what happened in both the past and the present in this dark tale. (Gr. 8–10) *See also* Mysteries in Time and Place—Mysterious Flashbacks and Time Travel.

Rosenfield, Kat. *Amelia Anne Is Dead and Gone.* **Dutton, 2012.**
Becca feels the pull of her small town during the summer after high school graduation, even as she longs to head to college. Her feelings toward her boyfriend, James, consume her thoughts and cloud her judgment as she joins the town in trying to learn what happened to a mysterious girl found dead on the road. Becca and others point fingers with dire results in this story for older teens that follows Becca's journey as well as the last days of victim Amelia Anne. (Gr. 10+)

Strasser, Todd. *Kill You Last* (The Thrillogy series). **Egmont, 2011.**
Nominated for an Edgar Award in 2011, this is the third title in Strasser's Thrillogy series about small-town Soundview. In each short volume, teens find themselves involved in crimes and looking for answers amid mounting danger. This installment features Shelby, whose father runs a photography business. When a few of her father's teen girl models go missing, the town turns on him, and Shelby learns their disgust is justified by his sleazy business practices. She also receives threatening texts warning her that she will be killed too if she keeps asking questions. This is a good one for reluctant readers. (Gr. 8–11)

▶ HUMOROUS INSPECTORS, OR WHAT'S SO FUNNY ABOUT CRIME?

Although there is nothing funny about murder, readers will enjoy the twist that humor brings to mystery stories. Many of these titles appeal to younger teen readers, but ironic and humorous voices are also appearing in mysteries for older teens.

Beaudoin, Sean. *You Killed Wesley Payne.* **Little, Brown, 2011.**
Dashiell Hammett hits high school in this modern-day noir. Dalton Rev is hired to find out who killed Wesley Payne and left his body hanging from the football goalpost. Although Dalton is attracted to the victim's sister, he tries to be a detective and sift emotion from fact amid the teeming cliques and lies. Humor and style make this book truly unique and fun for older teen readers. (Gr. 9–12)

Berk, Josh. *The Dark Days of Hamburger Halpin.* **Knopf, 2010.**
"Call me the Hefty Houdini." Will Halpin is deaf, but no dummy, like his infamous ancestor Dummy Halpin, who supposedly died in a cave-mining accident. When Will's high school class visits the same mine and a classmate is killed, Will wants to uncover the truth. Helping him is Hardy Boys fan Devon and ex-girlfriend Ebony. Although there is plenty of humor in the voice here, many things uncovered are far from humorous, including a tryst with a teacher, sexy photos of girls posted online, and more. This is a multilayered yet fun whodunit. (Gr. 6–9)

Ferraiolo, Jack D. *The Big Splash* **(Big Splash series). Amulet Books, 2011.**
Middle-school noir meets humor in this story of Matt Stevens, private detective, and the organized seventh-grade crime squad run by Vinny Biggs. The gang's biggest criminal act is soaking victims' pants with water guns filled with a variety of substances, and targets of this offense are "on the outs" with everyone. Matt is pulled into the criminal underworld during a case that has him experiencing jealousy and doubting friendships. This smart, funny mystery for younger teens is the first title in a series. (Gr. 5–7)

Jinks, Catherine. *The Reformed Vampire Support Group.* **Harcourt, 2009.**
Nina is eternally 15 years old, which is the age at which she became a vampire. But she hates being one—she is always feeling queasy, and worst of all she is stuck in a support group with annoying vampires who all try to keep each other from fanging people. But when one of their group is found staked, Nina knows she has to step out of her routine and risk her so-called life to find answers. Now is her chance to become like the superheroes she writes about. Great twists on the vampire genre with a mystery angle. Jinks followed up in 2010 with *The Abused Werewolf Rescue Group.* (Gr. 5–9) *See also* Fantastic and Paranormal Mysteries—Creatures with Clues.

Juby, Susan. *Getting the Girl: A Guide to Private Investigation, Surveillance and Cookery*. HarperTeen, 2008.
Freshman Sherman Mack wants to keep a low profile at his high school. He wants to do well in cooking class and admire crush Dini from afar. He wants nothing to do with the Defiling system at his school—if a girl's photo appears with a *D* in the bathrooms, the rest of the students act as if she is invisible. Lots of girls have transferred after being Defiled. Sherman realizes it is often the quieter girls who date popular boys who get Defiled. He worries about Dini after she starts seeing popular athlete Lester. When his mystery-loving friend Vanessa wants him to find out who is behind Defiling, Sherman reluctantly begins to track down clues. When Vanessa gets Defiled, he realizes he needs to take serious steps to stop the entire practice. (Gr. 6–9) For discussion suggestions, see chapter 6, "When Book Discussions Get Mysterious."

King, A. S. *Please Ignore Vera Dietz*. Knopf, 2010.
In this winner of the 2011 Michael L. Printz Honor Award, Vera is trying to ignore the ghost of her ex–best friend, Charlie, who visits her often as she goes about her pizza delivery job. She also tries to avoid thinking about the fight they had before he died and the secrets she knows about his death. While sorting through her grief, Vera realizes that true friendship does not change much in life or even afterward. (Gr. 9+) *See also* Fantastic and Paranormal Mysteries—Voices from the Beyond.

Leck, James. *The Adventures of Jack Lime*. Kids Can Press, 2010.
Jack Lime is a high school PI who really likes helping hot damsels in distress. He gets involved with a local gang of bullies and thieves, helps another teen avoid getting wedgies, and causes the prom king and queen to break up when he reveals the king's boyfriend. Funny and smart as Jack is, younger teen readers will know he is about to get his comeuppance in his last case as some folks turn the tables on him. (Gr. 5–7)

Low, Dene. *Petronella Saves Nearly Everyone: The Entomological Tales of Augustus T. Percival*. Houghton Mifflin, 2009. (Gr. 6–9)
See Mysteries in Time and Place—Historical Mysteries.

Moriarty, Jaclyn. *The Murder of Bindy MacKenzie*. Arthur A. Levine Books, 2006.
Smart girl Bindy has trouble with friendships and realizes many dislike her. She launches a campaign to change this situation through chapters of notes, letters, and humorous musings when she realizes someone is trying to kill her. She is not the only one involved in this far-reaching intrigue, however, and she is not sure whom to trust. Even her family is acting mysterious. She pieces together a conspiracy and tries to gain allies to combat it in this multilayered Australian story. (Gr. 6–9)

Pauley, Kimberly. *Cat Girl's Day Off*. Tu Books (Lee and Low), 2012.

Natalie has a lame talent in a family of geniuses: she can converse with cats. Only her two best friends know this secret. When she realizes a famous starlet's cat is asking for help while pictured on the news, Natalie and her friends grab the cat and try to learn what happened to the pet's owner. They encounter kidnapping and increasing danger as they work on a case no one would believe. (Gr. 7–10) *See also* Fantastic and Paranormal Mysteries—Supersleuths and Special Powers.

▶ SPORTY SLEUTHS

Sometimes a character's love of or involvement with a sport will place him or her in a unique situation for intrigue. Because sports are popular with teens, some may be attracted to mystery books through that angle.

Abrahams, Peter. *Bullet Point*. HarperTeen, 2010.

Budget cuts force aspiring baseball player Wyatt to move to another town, one closer to where his father is in prison. Wyatt falls for Greer, whose father is in the same prison, and soon the two teens decide to arrange a meeting between Wyatt and his dad. Doing so unleashes consequences Wyatt never imagined in this page-turner for older readers. (Gr. 9+) *See also* Thrillers—Thrilling Reading.

Abrahams, Peter. *Down the Rabbit Hole* (Echo Falls Mystery series). Harper-Collins, 2006. (Gr. 5–8)

See Realistic Mysteries—Small-Town Sleuths.

Bloor, Edward. *Tangerine: Tenth-Anniversary Edition*. Harcourt, 2007. (Gr. 6–10)

See High-Tech Whodunits—Futuristic Mysteries.

Bradbury, Jennifer. *Shift*. Atheneum, 2008. (Gr. 9+)

See Realistic Mysteries—Disappearing Family and Friends.

Feinstein, John. *Last Shot* (Final Four Mystery series). Knopf, 2005.

Winner of the 2006 Edgar Award, this title begins the sports-reporting investigations of junior high–age Steve Thomas and Susan Carol Anderson. Both win the opportunity to cover the games during the Final Four, but they end up writing about and solving a murder. This action-packed series takes readers from one famous sporting event to another. (Gr. 6+)

Parker, Robert. *The Boxer and the Spy*. Philomel, 2008. (Gr. 7–9)

See Realistic Mysteries—Small-Town Sleuths.

MYSTERIOUS BOOKTALKING EXAMPLES

The Morgue and Me by John C. Ford

Imagine that the only summer job you can find is at the town morgue. Now imagine that during your first day on the job, a body is brought in with five bullet holes in it and is labeled a suicide. Chris takes a picture of the body and decides to find out what really happened. What he finds out is that many people in his town are involved, even his best friend.

Following Christopher Creed by Carol Plum-Ucci

In *The Body of Christopher Creed*, a young man disappeared from a small town and was never seen again. In *Following Christopher Creed*, college reporter Mike wants to know what happened—to everyone. He finds a mother reviled by most of the town, a brother who has turned to substances and psychic means to connect with his missing sibling, and lots of trouble still lurking. Why did Chris really leave? Will he ever come back? Mike thinks the story will make his career, if it doesn't break him first.

COVERT MARKETING

Life in school is a bit like life in a small town. After promoting Small-Town Sleuth stories on a bookmark or website, invite students to write a paragraph describing what would most surprise them about a classmate or a teacher. Or post surprising things about willing teachers or students, or both, and see if teens can match the surprise to the person (for example, a teacher who won a cooking contest or a student whose short story was published).

HIGH-TECH WHODUNITS

The popularity of television shows with forensic-science themes over the past decade has fueled an avid interest in that career. Few authors are reaching teens specifically with forensics, but scientific approaches to the genre are increasingly popping up. Some are listed in this section in the CSI Teens category. Science fiction fans will also enjoy the Futuristic Mysteries. And the Internet, Computer, and Spy Capers category continues to be popular and appeals to thriller fans with high-speed, high-tech action.

Interview with EDWARD BLOOR

Edward Bloor worked as a teacher and a children's book editor before writing his own layered, complex, and engrossing books for young adult readers. *Tangerine* featured his interest in soccer. All of his popular and well-received books question reality in the future—and in the present.

Q: Several of your books feature mysteries and secrets. What are some of your favorite mystery authors (for teens or adults)?
A: I started out with Sherlock Holmes; I read all of those in a binge. I liked Robert B. Parker's Spenser books. I like that Frederick Forsyth includes a mystery and lots of nonfiction in his thrillers. I try to bend genres like that, too.

Q: How did you end up writing for young adults?
A: I got a job in educational publishing, where my assignment was to read young adult novels all day with an eye to excerpting them in a reading program. I had not heard of the genre, but I really liked it, and I saw an opportunity for myself to write in it.

Q: What did you like to read as a young adult?
A: I actually predate the genre, except for urtexts like *Catcher in the Rye*. I liked to read big, plot-heavy novels like *The Grapes of Wrath* and fact-based thrillers like *Fail Safe*.

Q: In *Tangerine*, Paul uncovers a family secret about his brother, Erik. In *Taken*, Charity also learns things about her family. Why do you think the theme of family secrets is so powerful for teens?
A: Because they know something is going on; they know they are not hearing the real story, or the full story, about their aunts, uncles, grandparents, and so on. Eventually, they do hear about that drug bust, or that trial separation, and so on.

Q: *Taken* is set in 2036, which is not all that far off in the future. What gave you the idea that kidnapping would be popular in the future?
A: It was a business trip I took to Cuernavaca, Mexico, for my publishing company. My host informed me that we would have to pay her through her bank account in Miami because, if it became known that she had a big contract with us, she might be kidnapped. I thought she was kidding, but she was not. Kidnapping was part of the local economy. I could think of no reason why that wouldn't happen here.

▶ CSI TEENS

Don't eat while reading these! Teen forensics books take a close—and descriptive—look at bodies, medicine, and death. Teens may be fascinated by the process and want to know more about this field.

Chibbaro, Julie. *Deadly*. Atheneum Books for Young Readers, 2011.
This historical mystery follows Prudence as she secures a job in a lab to get away from the School for Girls, where she knows she does not belong. Soon she is helping her mentor seek clues about the source of a disease. When each household with a death is found to have had the same cook, Prudence works to put together evidence against Typhoid Mary. This is an engrossing mystery with a strong heroine. (Grade 7+) *See also* Mysteries in Time and Place—Historical Mysteries.

Ferguson, Alane. *The Christopher Killer* (Forensic Mysteries series). Perfection Learning, 2008.
This first title in the series was nominated for an Edgar Award. The series features 17-year-old Cameryn, who helps her coroner father in Colorado. In the first book, she works to find the title serial killer using all her knowledge and forensic skill—before the killer finds her. (Gr. 8+)

Ford, John C. *The Morgue and Me*. Viking, 2009. (Gr. 10–12)
See Realistic Mysteries—Small-Town Sleuths.

Harazin, S. A. *Blood Brothers*. Delacorte, 2007.
This Edgar Award–nominated title follows 17-year-old med tech Clay, who is trying to scrape together money for rent and college while his best friend, Joey, is headed for an Ivy League premed school, courtesy of his parents. After a shift in the ER, Clay finds Joey disoriented and violent. Joey collapses into a coma at the hospital, and the police, wondering who gave Joey drugs, become interested in Clay. Clay is a loyal friend and uses all his knowledge to uncover what is happening to Joey. He also questions other teens to learn what really happened to his friend. Both the medical setting and Clay himself

are dynamic and unique, and this title will appeal to older teens. (Gr. 9+) For book discussion suggestions, see chapter 6, "When Book Discussions Get Mysterious."

Reichs, Kathy. *Virals* **(Virals series). Razorbill, 2010.**
Tory Brennan, niece of Reichs's star forensic scientist, Temperance, has the same interests as her aunt. In this first installment of the series, Tory and her new friends on an island off the coast of South Carolina find themselves investigating mysterious science experiments involving animals, as well as solving a cold case centering around a Vietnam War veteran. (Gr. 6–10)

Yancey, Rick. *The Monstrumologist* **(The Monstrumologist series). Simon and Schuster Books for Young Readers, 2010.**
This book is more horror than forensics, but the approach is the same, and science fans will enjoy it. Twelve-year-old Will Henry is an apprentice to a scientist who studies monsters, performing vividly described autopsies on them. It is soon clear that a mysterious and evil new creature is spreading, and Will must help stop the epidemic in this chilling historical tale. The first title was a Printz Honor Award selection. (Gr. 9+) *See also* Mysteries in Time and Place—Historical Mysteries.

▶ FUTURISTIC MYSTERIES

Teens wonder about what the future holds for them; these stories ponder intrigue in dark, futuristic conditions that extend the imagination in adrenalin-infused suspense.

Bloor, Edward. *Tangerine: Tenth-Anniversary Edition.* **Harcourt, 2007.**
In a town where lightning strikes at the same time every day, legally blind Paul can see that his brother, Erik, a football star, is involved in something terribly wrong. As he tries to find out what is going on, soccer player Paul uncovers even more troubling secrets in this surprise-filled story. (Gr. 6–10) *See also* Realistic Mysteries—Sporty Sleuths.

Haddix, Margaret Peterson. *FOUND* **(The Missing series). Simon and Schuster, 2009.**
A plane filled with babies is found at an airport. Thirteen years later, those children are receiving messages and unusual invitations. They want to know where they came from, even if the answer puts them right in the middle of conspiracy, time travel, and life-threatening danger. (Gr. 6+)

Henderson, J. A. *Bunker 10.* **Harcourt, 2007.**

Flashback mysteries begin with something terrible and work through what led up to that event. *Bunker 10* is no exception—it begins with an explosion in a room with seven teens. It turns out the teens live in a secret governmental lab. Some of them can't be trusted, as they have been part of an experiment gone bad. Personnel are on their way to wipe out anyone connected with the lab, but some of the teens want to save the group. A time machine enters the fray, and the adventure bends and rebends reality. (Gr. 7+) *See also* Mysteries in Time and Place—Mysterious Flashbacks and Time Travel.

Pearson, Mary. *The Adoration of Jenna Fox* **(The Jenna Fox Chronicles series). Henry Holt, 2008.**

Jenna wakes up after a year in a coma only to find she is literally not the same person. Her scientist father and mother decided to take the 10 percent of her brain that was left and rebuild her. There are new videos of her childhood and there are still the bodies of her two friends who also died in the accident, waiting to wake up as their new selves. The follow-up title, *The Fox Inheritance*, shows what happens when the teens wake up well into the future in these thought-provoking scientific thrillers. (Gr. 7+)

Roth, Veronica. *Divergent* **(Divergent series). Katharine Tegen Books, 2012. (Gr. 8+)**

See also Thrillers—Thrilling Reading.

Shusterman, Neal. *Unwind* **(Unwind Dystology series). Simon and Schuster Books for Young Readers, 2007. (Gr. 9+)**

See also Thrillers—Thrilling Reading.

▶ INTERNET, COMPUTER, AND SPY CAPERS

There is something so appealing about gadgets, international intrigue, and daredevil moves. It gets even better when the good-guy spies are teens themselves. Humor, action, and even romance can be found in these popular spy stories.

Carter, Ally. *I'd Tell You I Love You, but Then I'd Have to Kill You* **(Gallagher Girls series). Hyperion, 2007.**

The all-girl Gallagher Academy has some unusual classes, including martial arts, multiple languages, and state secrets. Cammie Morgan, daughter of a spy, knows she will follow in the family business, but what happens when she becomes attracted to a non-spy in the middle of a mission? (Gr. 7–10)

Child, Lauren. *Ruby Redfort: Look Into My Eyes.* **Candlewick, 2011.**
Child's popular Charlie and Lola series mentions Ruby Redfort books, starring a brilliant child code cracker. Now Ruby has her own title, and readers will enjoy the humorous techno-genius as they try to solve her code with her friend and the test she performs to join the Agency. She encounters villains and danger and keeps her cool in this fun mystery for younger teens. (Gr. 4–8)

Greenland, Shannon. *Model Spy* **(The Specialists series). Puffin, 2007.**
Computer genius Kelly is offered a chance to be part of a highly trained team of super spies. But life isn't always glamorous when solving international crimes. Those physical fitness training sessions aren't so hot, and Gigi, as she is now called, keeps learning more secrets about the parents she never knew. Each title in the series features another member of the Specialists team, but Gigi is a main character in all. (Gr. 6–9)

Horowitz, Anthony. *Stormbreaker* **(Alex Rider series). Philomel, 2001.**
The United States has the CIA. England has MI6. But when they fail, they have Alex Rider, teen spy. Excellent for younger boy or girl teens—loaded with action in this smart series. Younger fans will enjoy the graphic novel series of Alex Rider adventures for ages 10–14. Older fans will be ready for Ian Fleming's Bond series (ages 16+). (Gr. 5–9)

Jinks, Catherine. *Evil Genius* **(The Evil Genius series). Harcourt, 2007.**
Cadel Piggott is first caught hacking computers at age 7. His psychologist is an agent of the boy's super-evil father, who sends Cadel to the Axis Institute. Cadel enjoys studying embezzlement, among other skills, but stumbles upon someone good through his computer connections. Another agent at the evil school has a weapon of toxic BO, but also seems good. Cadel and his multitalented friends try to break out of the web of evil in the first of an amazing, high-tech suspense series. (Gr. 7+)

Patterson, James. *The Angel Experiment* **(Maximum Ride series). Little, Brown, 2005.**
Teens bred as part human and part bird escape the lab and fight for their lives and the lives of others in this fast-paced futuristic thriller series. Older teens will enjoy Patterson's Alex Cross series as well. (Gr. 7+)

Poznanski, Ursula. *Erebos.* **Annick Press, 2010.**
Nick is given a disc for an online role-playing game that pulls him in with riveting fights and challenges. Then the computer seems to know what he is doing when he is not playing, and soon it is sending him on missions in real life. He does not know whom to trust as he tries to find out about the game and its dark secrets in this international award–winning title. (Gr. 9+) For discussion suggestions, see chapter 6, "When Book Discussions Get Mysterious."

ADULT AUTHOR FOR TEENS: CHRISTOPHER REICH

Christopher Reich offers spy fiction with riveting action surrounding codes and capers. His Rules series features Dr. Jonathon Ransom, who is pulled into international intrigue after learning his wife was a spy before she died. Great for older teens looking for high-interest reading.

MYSTERIOUS BOOKTALKING EXAMPLES

Evil Genius by Catherine Jinks
What if you got caught hacking into a computer and your new psychologist told you, "Next time, don't get caught"? Imagine being sent to a school to learn how to commit identity theft, embezzlement, and other high-tech crimes. That may seem fun, but Cadel Piggott learns that the criminals who run the Axis Institute expect a lot in return.

Erebos by Ursula Poznanski
A friend gives Nick a disc for a new role-playing video game that has fun missions and a cool identity for him. But then the game asks him to recruit more players from the real world. When the game's leaders begin to question him about other things he is doing on the computer, Nick soon does not know whom he can trust online or in real life.

COVERT MARKETING

Old computer parts or discs scattered around a book display featuring futuristic mysteries or espionage stories add a tech edge, or at least look as if someone skilled has broken in to a computer—perhaps a spy. A running display of spy stories on a computer screen is another tie-in.

THRILLERS

It's all in the name—teen mysteries where the action ramps up and where every second counts. Time, deadlines, or shocking twists help define thrillers for teens. This category is not as clear-cut as Fantastic and Paranormal Mysteries, but teens who like high-octane reads may like these.

Interview with PETER ABRAHAMS

Noted author Peter Abrahams wrote Edgar Award–nominated suspense books for adults for many years before publishing *Down the Rabbit Hole* for younger teen readers (see Realistic Mysteries—Small-Town Sleuths), which was also nominated, though in a category new to him. Abrahams also took his trademark page-turning twists and suspense to older teens with *Reality Check* and *Bullet Point*, winning the 2010 Edgar Award for Young Adult books with *Reality Check*.

Q: What inspired you to start writing for younger readers after finding such success with your adult titles? Would you have been surprised when you started writing to know you'd have such success with both audiences?
A: Luckily for me, Laura Geringer at HarperCollins Children's read a book of mine called *The Tutor*, in which some of the scenes were written (in third-person close) from the POV of Ruby, a 10-year-old girl. Laura asked if I'd be interested in writing for younger readers. Off to the races! The other thing I had going for me was fatherhood—I've got four kids, so I'd seen just about everything. As for success, my reaction is not so much surprise as delight. Reading was so important to me as a kid, so it means a lot that I'm now on the supply side.

Q: What do you find easy and what do you find difficult about the younger audience?
A: The audience itself is nothing but a pleasure to write for. There's nothing jaded about the young imagination.

Q: How were reader reactions different for your Echo Falls titles than for your adult titles?
A: Younger readers seem more unbridled with their reactions! I get a lot of very interesting e-mail. Sometimes readers write whole Ingrid scenes of their own. Sometimes they're struggling with book reports (it was never my intention to add to their burden) and get the clever idea to go directly to the source. And there are some very moving e-mails, too, where something in the story has triggered thoughts about real problems in the reader's own life. Also, I get to go into schools sometimes, which I really enjoy. The kids seem to enjoy it too, if for no other reason than that it's a break in the endless routine.

Q: You have mentioned that you read Ross MacDonald as a teen but were disappointed when returning to them lately. What advice can you give teachers and librarians on inspiring teens to read mysteries?
A: Fantasy seems to be overwhelming all other genres at the moment. Perhaps mysteries could be recommended as something new and different, especially for those who've never read them. I believe there will always be a readership for exciting stories based in the real world.

Q: In _Reality Check_, the 2010 Edgar Award winner, you move to older teen readers with your classic psychological suspense. Cody does not know whom to trust as he sifts facts. Please tell readers about your inspiration for Cody and the missing Clea.
A: Following up on what I was saying about the real world, I've always been interested in class issues, something we don't often examine here in the United States, although we've certainly got them. Some people—like Clea—come into life with a solid foundation already waiting for them. For others—Cody, for example—crisis is just one or two slip-ups away. But then comes the question of what you're made of, or whether you can rise to the occasion. Those were some of the things on my mind as I began writing _Reality Check_. As for knowing whom to trust, that's in the very air we breathe in mystery writing, and one of the reasons I find the form so interesting.

Q: _Bullet Point_ also includes an older boy teen, Wyatt, who has trouble finding people who are trustworthy, right up until the last page, when the true colors of those around him are shown. What do you hope readers will find in this book?
A: _Bullet Point_ is darker than _Reality Check_, in fact, one of the noirest books I've written. More and more I've come to believe that you shouldn't pull punches, that the writer shouldn't pander to any perceived expectations of the reader. I trust the taste and intellect of the reader. _Bullet Point_ is for readers looking for a gritty, even gut-wrenching, experience. Bad things do happen and are not always preventable.

Q: What are you working on for adult readers?
A: Under my pen name, Spencer Quinn, I write the Chet and Bernie series. Number six, _The Sound and the Furry_, was published in September 2013. These are private-eye novels narrated by Chet, the canine partner of Bernie Little, PI. Chet is not a talking dog, or a human in a dog costume; he's 100 percent dog, with all the attendant limitations (and strengths). Chet's blog: chetthedog.com.

❱ THRILLING READING

Abrahams, Peter. _Bullet Point_. HarperTeen, 2010. (Gr. 9+)
    See Realistic Mysteries—Sporty Sleuths.

Abrahams, Peter. *Reality Check.* **HarperTeen, 2010.**
This winner of the 2010 Edgar Award will hold readers captive until the last page. An injury has benched Cody, ruining his scholarship chances and causing him to drop out of school. When his girlfriend, Clea, goes missing from her Vermont boarding school, Cody gets involved in the search. The school's small-town locale is filled with surprise villains and secrets, and Cody's fresh perspective cuts through to find clues in this riveting read. (Gr. 8–11) *See also* Realistic Mysteries— Disappearing Family and Friends.

Cadnum, Michael. *Seize the Storm.* **Farrar, Straus and Giroux, 2012.**
In this taut suspense novel, a family yacht outing for cousins, adults, and some crew turns sinister when they come across a boat with two bodies and a large sum of money. Not only is the family now hunted by the killers, but greed is threatening to break up the group from within. (Gr. 9+)

Cooney, Caroline B. *Diamonds in the Shadow.* **Waterbrook Press, 2007.**
In this Edgar Award–nominated title, Jared Finch is annoyed when his family takes in African refugees. The family brings little except some ashes, within which Jared and his sister find uncut diamonds. Cooney keeps the plot moving with danger and suspense while subtly highlighting the terrible life people are enduring in the region. (Gr. 9+)

Evans, Richard Paul. *Michael Vey: The Prisoner of Cell 25* **(Michael Vey series). Mercury Ink/Simon Pulse, 2011.**
Michael has Tourette's syndrome, which can be challenging, but his real secret is that he can zap people with electricity. Another teen sees him use his power when he is fighting bullies, and soon he realizes there are others with unusual electrical powers. Seventeen babies were given these powers in a science experiment, and now those who created their powers want them back—to eliminate them. This well-crafted series has a hero teens will relate to amid a fantastic scientific plot. (Gr. 6+) *See also* High-Tech Whodunits— Supersleuths and Special Powers.

Giles, Gail. *What Happened to Cass McBride?* **Little, Brown, 2007.**
Cass is popular and likes to stomp those who aren't. Kyle's brother committed suicide, and Kyle wants revenge against someone he felt helped cause it. He traps Cass underground in a box and communicates with her through a straw. As the teens talk and learn more about each other, readers will be aware of time running out in this powerful story. (Gr. 9+)

Price, Charlie. *Desert Angel.* **Farrar, Straus and Giroux, 2011.**
Fourteen-year-old Angel wakes up to find her mother murdered and her mother's boyfriend, Scotty, gone. Scotty is an expert tracker who will not want her as a witness, and Angel flees into the desert with few supplies or ideas on how to survive. (Gr. 9+)

Roth, Veronica. *Divergent* **(Divergent series). Katharine Tegen Books, 2012.**
Beatrice has to choose her life from among five personality factions in this dystopian Chicago future. She eschews her family's Abnegation role and joins Dauntless, where she must perform a series of grueling psychological and physical tests to ascertain her bravery. As she climbs her way through, she realizes some things about the system are lies, and a force seems to be leading the factions into war. Teens and adults will enjoy this unique, unsettling, and highly suspenseful ride. (Gr. 8+) *See also* High-Tech Whodunits—Futuristic Mysteries.

Sedgwick, Marcus. *White Crow.* **Roaring Brook Press, 2011.**
Like *The Monstrumologist* in tone, *White Crow* combines spine-tingling suspense, history, and gothic evil into a thriller for horror and mystery fans. Modern-day Rebecca resents being taken by her father to spend a boring summer in a town that seems to be slipping into the sea, but is stunned when she encounters the mysterious and elfin Ferelith, who knows a lot about the dark past of Winterfold Hall. Their story is overlaid by excerpts from tales of an evil visitor and experiments, written by a rector in 1790. (Gr. 10+)

Shusterman, Neal. *Unwind* **(Unwind Dystology series). Simon and Schuster Books for Young Readers, 2007.**
In the future, abortion will be outlawed, but unwinding will be allowed. This practice allows parents to have their teenage children's organs harvested to help others. Three teens meet on the way to the harvest camps. One was raised to be harvested. One was too hard for his parents to handle. One was a result of budget cuts, as she was not talented enough to become a professional musician. This one will warp readers' minds while they hurry to find out if the three survive. (Gr. 9+) *See also* High-Tech Whodunits—Futuristic Mysteries.

Smith, Alexander Gordon. *Lockdown* **(Escape from Furnace series). Farrar, Straus and Giroux, 2009.**
When Alex and his friend are caught by strange individuals during a house burglary, the friend is murdered, and Alex is taken to a prison below the surface of the earth. The conditions are terrible and shocking, and the series' cliffhangers will make readers want more. (Gr. 9+)

Wynne-Jones, Tim. *Blink and Caution.* **Candlewick, 2011.**
Blink stumbles upon a kidnapping and becomes obsessed with rescuing the victim. Caution is another runaway who thinks she can scam Blink. Instead he persuades her to join him, and they both soon find themselves in danger. (Gr. 9+)

MYSTERIOUS BOOKTALKING EXAMPLES

Michael Vey: The Prisoner of Cell 25 **by Richard Paul Evans**
What good would it do you to have a special power with which you could zap people with electricity? What would you do with that? Michael Vey has never let anyone see his power. To everyone at school, he is the kid with Tourette's syndrome. He does have that, too, but the power singles him out. When someone spots him using it, he learns that there are others. Sixteen others. And the folks who gave all of them this power want them all back.

Unwind **by Neal Shusterman**
Who knows what organ donation is? What if it wasn't a choice? Meet Connor, Lev, and Risa, who are on their way to be unwound. "Unwinding" means giving organs for other teens to use. They do not want to die. They may not have a choice.

COVERT MARKETING

Set up a stopwatch or timer-themed objects around the thriller books. Use posters or other signs with the words *hurry* or *rush* or *now* to encourage readers to find out how these characters save themselves.

FANTASTIC AND PARANORMAL MYSTERIES

Although a fine line separates types of fantasy, there are distinct elements and trends that fans will appreciate. In one type of story, teens can solve mysteries thanks in part to a special power. In other tales, dark forces or other people with special powers permeate the adventure and make life very difficult for the sleuths. Sometimes the victims or other ghosts tell stories after they die to find justice. And in more traditional paranormal tales, supernatural creatures hold sway. Why not just make one list that includes all types of paranormal mysteries? Presenting them together may encourage teens to try new authors and titles.

Interview with CHRIS GRABENSTEIN

After writing award-winning adult mysteries for a few years, Chris Grabenstein published *The Crossroads* about Zack, who learns that he can see and talk to people others cannot. This humorous series combines paranormal and suspense, producing an Anthony Award–winning result. Chris now writes the Riley Mack series for younger readers as well.

Q: What did you like to read as a teen?
A: I loved reading *Mad* magazine and *Mad* books. I've had a subscription since I was 10 years old. *Mad* taught me about satire/sarcasm and writing funny. I, of course, read all the books they made us read at school. I loved Edgar Allan Poe and the short stories of O. Henry. When I got to high school, I quickly fell in love with Shakespeare and anyone who wrote a play!

Q: How did you get started writing mysteries for adults?
A: After writing advertising copy for almost twenty years, I quit my job as an executive VP and group creative director at Young and Rubicam and locked myself in a spare bedroom for four years where I wrote screenplays, scary novels, thrillers, and mysteries—all the books I had loved reading during my advertising career on those long trips between New York and Los Angeles. I loved page-turners that made the six-hour flight (pardon the pun) fly by. My first published mystery (*Tilt-a-Whirl*) was actually the fourth book I had written. And I have boxes and boxes of rejected screenplays gathering dust in my storage space!

Q: What led you to write for younger readers?
A: A lot of my nieces and nephews wanted to read one of my books. Since the Ceepak mysteries contain what HBO always calls "adult language and situations," they couldn't read any of those mysteries. And my two thrillers were even darker. So, when an editor asked if I could turn an unpublished, 120,000-word ghost story called *The Crossroads* into a 50,000-word middle grades book, I jumped at the chance. Best decision I ever made. I love the fact that the book won starred reviews

and awards. But what I really love is the incredible new audience of middle school readers I discovered.

Q: What led you to write a paranormal series with Zack?
A: I think Zack is a lot like me when I was 11. Sort of shy. A boy with a big imagination and not many friends. A kid whom the bullies pick on. But then he gets a fantastic stepmother who helps him blossom into the kid he was always meant to be. The first book in the Haunted Mystery series, *The Crossroads*, is really a rumination on grief. What do you do after someone dies? Mourn them forever or move on with your life. The wicked Gerda Spratling makes one choice in the book. Zack, with the help of Judy and his new friend Davy, takes a different course and heads further on up the road.

Q: You now write or co-write several series for younger readers, plus a stand-alone title coming. What do you see in the future for Riley and Zack?
A: Well, I just completed the manuscript for *Riley Mack II*. Right now we're calling it *Riley Mack Stirs Up More Trouble*. In it, Riley and his crew of "known troublemakers" solve the mystery of what is polluting their favorite swimming hole and take down a crooked corporate tycoon. The series is an *Ocean's Eleven* for 11-year-olds.

Over at Random House, we're taking a break from the Haunted Mystery series to concentrate on a stand-alone (or maybe it might become a series) called *Escape from Mr. Lemoncello's Library*. It's a puzzle mystery. Twelve 12-year-olds get locked inside the most magnificent and magical public library ever created. The billionaire game maker Luigi Lemoncello invites them to play a new game: find your way out of the library by using information you find inside the library.

Q: What are some of your favorite fan reactions? How are they different from adult fans?
A: My absolute favorite reactions are the kids who come to library events hugging my books. Adults do not do this. I, of course, love the e-mails that tell me that my books are the best "I have ever read in my whole life." And, I particularly love the e-mails from parents who tell me their son or daughter had not read a book in years and couldn't put mine down.

Q: What can libraries best do to promote teen mysteries?
A: I think it would be neat to have the teens write their own interactive mystery skit after they have read a few and figure out how the puzzles work. One library I have visited does this. They told me the kids had a blast. Also, I hope libraries will let teens play puzzle games similar to the one I concocted for *Escape from Mr. Lemoncello's Library*. It would be fun to have teens compete to find something hidden in the library by using a string of "Dewey decimal" clues.

Q: What do you do at school visits?
A: Have a blast! For fourth through sixth graders, I try to teach a little bit about

story mapping and structure through a fun and interactive presentation. I walk the kids through *The Crossroads*, explaining setting, protagonist, antagonist, and conflict in a way that makes it fun. Then, using their shouted-out suggestions, we build a new story map for a brand-new ghost story that I improvise on the spot. (Yes, I spent my early 20s doing improvisational comedy with the likes of Bruce Willis and Kathy Kinney down in Greenwich Village, so I am a trained professional. Do not attempt to make up stories on the spot at home.)

For older kids, seventh and eighth grades, I demonstrate the rules of improv comedy and how to use them when writing. Usually, when I'm done, the kids go running out of the auditorium eager to start writing! I try to make writing something that's fun to do, not a painful exercise in grammar and punctuation.

❱ SUPERSLEUTHS AND SPECIAL POWERS

Special powers can be a big help when solving crimes, but sometimes those powers also interfere with teen life.

Bray, Libba. *The Diviners*. Little, Brown, 2012. (Gr. 9+)
See Mysteries in Time and Place—Historical Mysteries.

Cusick, Richie Tankersley. *Spirit Walk: Walk of the Spirits and Shadow Mirror*. Speak, 2013.
The publisher combines two earlier titles in one here with *Spirit Walk*. The stories feature Miranda, who, after moving to history-steeped St. Yvette, Louisiana, discovers she can get messages from ghosts and help them. She meets her grandfather for the first time in *Walk of the Spirits* and learns he had that ability as well, though he was considered crazy right up until his death. Miranda becomes friends with several teens who help her solve the mysteries, piecing together the clues from the ghosts. One friend, Etienne, becomes more than just a friend, though his secrets come between them in *Shadow Mirror*. (Gr. 8–10) *See also* Romantic Suspense.

Derting, Kimberly. *The Body Finder* (The Body Finder Novels series). Harper, 2010.
Finding a dead girl at age 8 was weird for Violet, but what was weirder was that she had been sensing the presence of untimely death her entire life. She knew when animals killed by predators were underground, and she sensed an imprint of sorts—color or taste on people who had brought about the death of another. Now as a teen, all she wants to think about is her changing feelings for longtime best friend Jay and not how she just found another body— another girl in a lake. Then more girls disappear. It has to stop, and this time Violet chooses to find the killer. (Gr. 9+) *See also* Romantic Suspense.

Evans, Richard Paul. *Michael Vey: The Prisoner of Cell 25* (Michael Vey series). Mercury Ink/Simon Pulse, 2011. (Gr. 6+)
See Thrillers—Thrilling Reading.

Gier, Kerstin. *Ruby Red* (Ruby Red series). Henry Holt, 2011. (Gr. 6–9)
See Mysteries in Time and Place—Mysterious Flashbacks and Time Travel.

Harrington, Kim. *Clarity* (Clarity Novels series). Point, 2011.
Clare gets visions from things she touches. Her mother and brother also have special abilities. Although the three of them have been long regarded as freaks in their small town, Clare is now asked to help after a young woman is murdered. She teams with the son of a detective to solve crimes after her brother becomes a suspect in the first title of this page-turning paranormal mystery series. (Gr. 7+)

Hodkin, Michelle. *The Unbecoming of Mara Dyer* (The Mara Dyer Trilogy). Simon and Schuster, 2011.
When Mara wakes in a hospital, she has no idea how she got there. She learns that she was in a pocket of air when an abandoned building collapsed on her and three friends. Her family moves to make a fresh start, but Mara is treated for psychotic episodes when she sees the dead teens. Her bad feeling about a Spanish teacher before the teacher is found dead convinces her that she has terrible powers. At the same time she is falling in love with Noah, who seems to understand her. The two try to learn about the source of their powers in this first title of the series. (Gr. 9+) *See also* Romantic Suspense.

Johnson, Maureen. *The Name of the Star* (The Shades of London series). Putnam, 2011.
In this Edgar Award–nominated title, Louisiana teen Rory heads to a London boarding school just as Jack the Ripper copycat crimes are occurring. She sees a mysterious man no one else can see, and after she reports it, special agents come to talk with her. She uses her talent with paranormal forces to solve the crimes in this highly suspenseful mystery. (Gr. 7+)

Layman, John, and Rob Guillory. *Chew: Volume 1, Taster's Choice* (Chew series). Image Comics, 2009.
Detective Tony Chu can get visions and impressions from his food and uses that ability to solve crimes, though it does mean he has to eat some unpleasant things. This graphic novel series for older teens is zany but with a police procedural approach. (Gr. 10+)

McMann, Lisa. *Wake* **(Wake Trilogy). Simon Pulse, 2008.**
Beyond her control, 17-year-old Janie gets pulled into people's dreams. She decides to stop driving, as it happens then. She ends up in disturbing visions and begins to realize she can use her talent to help others. When she is pulled into a dream about a crime, she tries to uncover clues. But this talent takes a heavy toll. Even with the help of her handsome neighbor, Janie will not be the same person after the dreams. (Gr. 9+)

Olsen, Greg. *Envy* **(Empty Coffin series). Splinter, 2011.**
In their small town of Port Gamble, known as Empty Coffin, twins Hayley and Taylor do not believe the death of their friend Katelyn was suicide as rumored. The twins use some telepathy and their brain power to learn more about what happened in this first title of the series, based on a real cyberbullying case. (Gr. 7–10)

Pauley, Kimberly. *Cat Girl's Day Off.* **Tu Books (Lee and Low), 2012. (Gr. 7–10)**
See Realistic Mysteries—Humorous Inspectors, or What's So Funny about Crime?

Perez, Marlene. *Dead Is the New Black* **(Dead Is series). Graphia, 2008.**
Daisy is the only Giordano sister without a psychic power. But she still knows something is going on with cheerleader Samantha, something undead. Daisy goes undercover and, in the process of solving the crime, learns she does have some special abilities. Daisy and her family provide humor, mystery, and even a little romance in this fun series. (Gr. 7+)

Staub, Wendy Corsi. *Lily Dale Awakening* **(Lily Dale series). Walker, 2007.**
After her mother dies in an accident, Calla has to move in with her psychic grandmother in the odd town of Lily Dale. She quickly becomes aware that she also has special abilities and that her mother's death may not have been an accident. And Calla may be the next target. Smart, clever Calla leads readers into this dark, paranormal series. (Gr. 7–10)

Ward, Rachel. *Numbers* **(Numbers series). Chicken House, 2010.**
Fifteen-year-old Jem has always been able to see numbers on people's foreheads. The numbers are the date of their death. She can't see her own, even in a mirror. When she and a friend cut school to ride the London Eye ferris wheel, she realizes that everyone in line has the same date—today. As Jem and her friend escape a terrorist plot, they become suspects. A highly suspenseful, unique series for older teen readers. (Gr. 9+)

ADULT SUPERSLEUTH AND SPECIAL POWERS TITLES FOR TEENS

Fforde, Jasper. *The Eyre Affair* (Thursday Next Novels series). Viking, 2002.
Thursday Next is from the Literary Division of the Special Operations Network charged with hunting down the killer of book characters. Hades, the villain, enters books and steals or murders famous characters. Paranormal and humorous elements are woven through titles and authors teens may meet in high school but might enjoy more in this form. (Gr. 9+)

Hamilton, Steve. *The Lock Artist*. Minotaur Books, 2010.
Edgar-winner Hamilton introduces readers to Mike Smith, who can't speak but who can open any lock, safe, or padlock. He has been in prison for that talent, but now is out and trying to avoid a bad guy. As he travels, he drops clues about how he lost his ability to speak. (Gr. 9+)

Laurie, Victoria. *Abby Cooper, Psychic Eye* (Psychic Eye Mysteries series).
  Signet, 2004.
Psychic Abby is upset that she did not foresee the death of one of her clients. The lead investigator is handsome and doubtful of her abilities, even when she ferrets out liars and criminals in this smart, believable series. (Gr. 9+)

▌ DARK FORCES

Paranormal forces can be dark and deadly. Teens in these stories have to work against often unseen forces that are trying to herd them into danger.

Dashner, James. *The Maze Runner* (Maze Runner series). Delacorte, 2009.
  Thomas wakes up in an elevator and emerges, only to enter a maze, where other teens welcome him. As he tries to figure out how to leave the maze, he realizes that another boy arrives every thirty days. He and the others survive by working the land and using all their skills in this series with cliff-hanging endings for each title. (Gr. 6+)

Ford, Michael. *The Poisoned House*. Albert Whitman, 2011.
  In 1950s London, 15-year-old servant Abi does not understand the mysterious happenings in the house. Handprints appear, messages come through botched séances and Ouija boards, and Abi begins to wonder if her own dead mother is trying to warn her of danger. Gothic spine-tingling reading for fans of that style. (Gr. 8+) *See also* Mysteries in Time and Place—Historical Mysteries.

Healey, Karen. *The Shattering*. Little, Brown, 2011.
  Keri is reeling from her brother Jake's suicide when an old friend suggests that it was murder. Keri, Janna, and Sione all lost their brothers to suicide,

and as they begin to investigate the deaths, they realize that many boys fit a pattern, but some do not. They also realize that nothing ever goes wrong in their small Australian town, and perhaps some dark forces are keeping it that way—forces that require some murder. (Gr. 9+)

McMann, Lisa. *Cryer's Cross.* **Simon Pulse, 2011.**
Kendall Fletcher tries to be a normal teen even though she lives in a tiny town with a one-room schoolhouse and she has severe OCD. First a girl goes missing in the town, then Kendall's best friend, Nico, disappears. She can barely keep herself going through her grief, but two new students work to pull her together and find out what happened. Mysterious writing on a desk shows them something sinister befell the teens, and Kendall must battle dark forces before they can get her, too. (Gr. 8+)

Miller, Barnabas, and Jordan Orlando. *7 Souls.* **Random House Children's Books, 2010. (Gr. 9+)**
See Mysteries in Time and Place—Mysterious Flashbacks and Time Travel.

Mitchell, Saundra. *Shadowed Summer.* **Delacorte, 2009.**
In this Edgar Award–nominated title, 14-year-old Iris thinks her small-town summer is going to be boring. A whisper in her ear makes her think she is hearing from a boy who disappeared from the town twenty years ago. As she learns more, she realizes that someone else wants that story to remain a secret. (Gr. 8+)

Suma, Nova Ren. *Imaginary Girls.* **Dutton, 2011.**
Chloe lives with her sister, Ruby, and loves everything about their relaxed life. Then one night Ruby's friends dare Chloe to swim far out on the lake, and she finds a body floating in a boat. Chloe is then sent to live with the father she barely knows. Months later, Ruby comes for her and brings her back to their small town. Chloe knows something is weird when the girl she found dead on the lake seems to be alive and hanging out with Ruby. Then she learns that there are creatures living under the lake, and Ruby has made a deal with them. The interesting paranormal twist will appeal to mystery readers who like some supernatural with their suspense. (Gr. 8+)

Wooding, Chris. *Malice* **(Malice series). Scholastic, 2010.**
Malice is a sinister comic book overseen by Tall Jake. Luke, Seth, and Kady do not believe the rumors that children disappear into the comic, until Luke is trapped. The others follow and try to figure out how to survive in this graphic novel series. (Gr. 9+)

❱ VOICES FROM THE BEYOND

These stories are similar to the selections in the Supersleuths and Special Powers category, but the crimes here are solved because of what the dead have to say, and the special abilities of the sleuths involve speaking with the departed.

Armstrong, Kelly. *The Summoning* **(Darkest Powers series). HarperCollins, 2008.**
Chloe is imprisoned in a group home for troubled teens when she meets her first ghost. The ghost helps her learn more about the dark past of Lyle House, including supernatural secrets. Armstrong brings her skill for fast-paced supernatural stories to teens in this series. (Gr. 6+)

Grabenstein, Chris. *The Crossroads* **(Haunted Mystery series). Yearling Books, 2008.**
When Zack, his father, and his new stepmother move to the country, Zack does not understand why so many people are hanging around the tree in his front yard. Then he realizes not everyone can see them, or talk to them, as he does. Soon it is obvious that some living people are interested in the tree as well, and Zack begins to investigate why the tree is so important. Zack's abilities pull him into mysteries in different locations throughout the series, from school to a haunted theater and more. Ghosts, humor, mysteries, and a relatable Zack make this series a winner for reluctant readers. (Gr. 6–8)

Griffin, Adele, and Lisa Brown. *Picture the Dead.* **Sourcebooks Fire, 2010. (Gr. 7+)**
See Mysteries in Time and Place—Historical Mysteries.

King, A. S. *Please Ignore Vera Dietz.* **Knopf, 2010.**
See Realistic Mysteries—Humorous Inspectors, or What's So Funny about Crime?

Maguire, Eden. *Beautiful Dead: Jonas* **(Beautiful Dead series). Sourcebooks Fire, 2010.**
Each title in this four-book series centers on one of the four teens from the same high school who have been killed. In this first book, Darina is grief-stricken after her boyfriend, Phoenix, is stabbed to death. She encounters the four teens and learns they each have only a year to resolve what happened to them. Jonas has only four days left before his deadline. Darina agrees to help so she can be with Phoenix, even though the bargain means the loss of her memory. (Gr. 8+)

Price, Charlie. *Dead Connection*. **Roaring Brook Press, 2006.**
Murray Kiefer likes to hang out at the cemetery because he can communicate with those buried there. It beats high school. But one day he hears the voice of a missing cheerleader coming from one of the graves. The cemetery caretaker's daughter, Pearl, becomes an unwilling partner in a detecting duo that defies a myriad of adult limitations and interesting characters to seek justice. (Gr. 6–9)

Riggs, Ransom. *Miss Peregrine's Home for Peculiar Children*. **Quirk Books, 2011.**
A family tragedy sends Jacob to a remote island off the coast of Wales, where he learns more about Miss Peregrine's Home. Island natives insist all the children died decades ago, but to Jacob they seem alive. The photography and eerie theme of this book will captivate readers from the beginning. (Gr. 9+) *See also* Mysteries in Time and Place—Historical Mysteries.

Stolarz, Laurie Faria. *Project 17*. **Hyperion, 2007.**
Danvers State Hospital, known for its use of the lobotomy in the many decades before it was closed, seems like the perfect place for Derik and his friends to film a movie throughout an entire night before the facility is demolished. Instead, through ghostly clues and the number seventeen, they are drawn into the mysteries of the patients and the medical procedures they endured. Fans of *Ghost Hunters* and similar television shows will recognize the facility and style of this book. (Gr. 8+)

Warman, Jessica. *Between*. **Walker, 2011.**
Elizabeth Valchar wakes up on a yacht during her eighteenth birthday party hearing a thumping noise. It turns out to be her own body floating in the water. She is met by Alex, the ghost of another teen from her high school who died in a hit-and-run. She can't remember at first what happened to her, but soon Alex takes her through her memories to help her piece together some of the secrets that led to her death. (Gr. 9–12) *See also* Mysteries in Time and Place—Mysterious Flashbacks and Time Travel.

▶ CREATURES WITH CLUES

Vampires, werewolves, angels, and more have become common and popular in teen fiction. In these books, teens who are creatures or who encounter them help solve crimes.

Beaudoin, Sean. *Infects*. **Candlewick, 2012.**
Nick "Nero" Sole is forced to go on an Inward Trek with other delinquents that turns deadly after the counselors turn into flesh-eating monsters. The

teens use everything they know from monster movies to fight the creatures, only to realize that they do not know who the real bad guy is. (Gr. 9+)

Bowler, Tim. *Buried Thunder.* **Holiday House, 2011.**
Maya is led into the forest by a fox's eyes, only to find three bodies. But no one else sees the bodies, and she is labeled a troublemaker in the small English town to which her family has just moved. The hotel they run seems to inspire some fear and gossip in the town's residents, and mysterious things are happening. Maya hears scratching and feels as though she is being watched. Some locals are threatening, and some are plain weird, but it becomes clear that something dark is occurring when a real body is found. Maya works to find out what is happening even as danger closes in on her. (Gr. 5–8)

Jinks, Catherine. *The Reformed Vampire Support Group.* **Harcourt, 2009. (Gr. 5–9)**
See Realistic Mysteries—Humorous Inspectors, or What's So Funny about Crime?

Peacock, Kathleen. *Hemlock* **(Hemlock series). HarperCollins, 2012.**
In this first book of a planned trilogy, MacKenzie is still trying to manage months after her best friend, Amy, was murdered by a werewolf in their small town of Hemlock. Amy's boyfriend Jason's behavior has turned dark, and Kyle, the fourth in their group, is also being mysterious. A tracker group moves into town to kill the werewolves, but Mac's dreams about Amy tell her that is the wrong answer. Mac is attacked by a tracker, who threatens her to not talk about it. She is also saved by a werewolf that turns out to be someone she knows. Mac's desire to find out what happened to her friend while sorting through her romantic feelings for Kyle and her confused feelings for Jason make this story a realistic, engrossing teen tale. (Gr. 7+) *See also* Romantic Suspense. For discussion suggestions, see chapter 6, "When Book Discussions Get Mysterious."

Taylor, Laini. *Daughter of Smoke and Bone* **(Daughter of Smoke and Bone series). Little, Brown, 2011.**
Karou has to perform unexplained errands all over the world to collect teeth for her mysterious adoptive father. She realizes an angel is tracking her, and she learns that she comes from the Chimera race. Her adoptive family disappears before they can answer her questions. This vivid, rich fantasy offers unique creatures and elements, and readers will sympathize with both the good and the bad sides. This first book in the series leaves questions unanswered, but readers will be entranced. (Gr. 9+)

Weston, Robert Paul. *Dust City.* **Razorbill, 2010.**

This Edgar Award–nominated title turns fairy tales on their heads as it follows the story of Henry Whelp, who is next in line to be the Big Bad Wolf. His father is currently in prison for the double murders of Little Red Riding Hood and her grandmother. When another crime forces Henry from the Home for Wayward Wolves, he realizes his father was framed and sniffs out the clues to clear him. (Gr. 7–10)

MYSTERIOUS BOOKTALKING EXAMPLES

Please Ignore Vera Dietz by A. S. King

Vera's best friend, Charlie, changed before he died. He became interested in new things and people, and, in her hurt, they argued. After his death, Charlie begins to haunt Vera, encouraging her to find out what happened to him. Most people think it was an accident. Vera does not know what to believe.

Project 17 by Laurie Faria Stolarz

Would you like to spend an entire night in an abandoned mental hospital? After graduation, Derik and his friends decide to make a film in the haunted Danvers State Hospital before it is torn down. They get clues about the number seventeen and the patients who lived and died at Danvers. The hospital was real and known for lobotomies among other dark practices.

COVERT MARKETING

Mysterious creature tracks leading to a display of titles of paranormal mysteries will get attention. A trivia sheet inviting teens to match the special power to the character is another way to engage them with these titles.

MYSTERIES IN TIME AND PLACE

Historical mysteries pull readers into adventures where setting and time become important elements and clues. Certain periods become trends in publishing, as do famous sleuths such as James Bond and Sherlock Holmes. Teens who enjoy reading about different times may also enjoy flashback mysteries, cold cases, and mysteries set in other lands. All pull the reader out of the ordinary in unique ways that realistic mysteries do not.

Interview with JULIE HYZY

Chicago-area author Julie Hyzy is best known for her White House Chef and her Manor House Mystery series. Since *State of the Onion* was published in 2008, the adventures of Ollie in the White House have garnered several awards, including the Anthony and readers' awards. Ollie's stories are set in modern times but are steeped in the history and traditions of the United States, as seen from the White House. Readers learn about holiday traditions, protocol for state dinners, and even foods and dishes. Hyzy's Manor House Mystery series features Grace, who is in charge of programs at Marshfield Manor, a southern tourist estate. Readers learn about many elements of history, including the Civil War era. Hyzy's titles have been listed in *Voice of Youth Advocates'* annual article of adult mysteries for teens, as they are filled with action, history, and light romance. Readers can learn more about Julie Hyzy at www.juliehyzy.com.

Q: Your mystery series consistently appear on lists of titles with appeal for young adults. Why do you think Ollie, for example, appeals to high school mystery fans? Do you think having teens at home while writing your series (especially the early ones) built in appeal?
A: I hadn't thought about that, but now that you bring it up, I'm sure having my teenage daughters home while writing the series helped shape my stories and even shape Ollie. The teenagers I've gotten to know have all been bright, bold, strong-minded, and optimistic. I like to think that Ollie shares those traits as well. I'm absolutely delighted to know that readers of all ages are enjoying the books.

Q: What did you like to read when you were in high school?
A: I wasn't crazy about our reading assignments—I found the books teachers chose to be dry and boring. Maybe I just didn't give those books a fair chance. I chose to read short stories by Ray Bradbury (*loved* that man!) and other classics that weren't assigned, like *To Kill a Mockingbird*. I read mysteries and romances, too. Couldn't get enough of those.

Q: The White House Chef series especially brings history to life for your readers. What do you think teens would be interested to discover about Washington, DC, from your books that they would not get from their history books?
A: What I found the most interesting about life in the White House is that the president and family are not insulated from the staff. There's a warm, cordial relationship there. Staffers leave their politics at the door—their goal is to be the best they can be, whether that is chef, butler, usher, or maintenance engineer. I like to emphasize that attitude in the books. It's pretty awesome.

Q: Grace also interacts with history, especially with the Civil War era, at her mansion. What do you enjoy about research for both series?
A: Everything about the White House is fun and interesting, and whenever I can uncover a new tidbit, it's like gold.

What I really like about the Grace (Manor House Mysteries) series is that she's the person in charge and doesn't have to worry about the Secret Service watching her every move. That's fun and freeing. I adore researching Grace's series because that gives me an excuse to tour mansions all over the world. Every home has a story and secrets. Grace's Marshfield is no exception. Touring some of the fabulous places in the United States and elsewhere gives me ideas for lots more intrigue.

Q: What can libraries do, in your opinion, to stay relevant and appealing to teen readers?
A: Offering a welcoming environment is key. Teenagers like to be heard, like to believe their opinions count. Heck, everybody wants that. Libraries have an open-door policy, and that's great. Having librarians who enjoy working with teens is great. But sometimes (I've seen it) staff members who don't particularly love working with teens need to learn that the kids hanging out at the library probably aren't the troublemakers. It would be nice to cut those kids some slack. The more teens are at the library, the more they're probably learning. That's the best. And it actually applies to everyone. Learning is lifelong.

Q: What advice would you have for teen writers?
A: Write every day. Read every day. Read outside of your comfort zone. Make sure you know the rules—grammar and spelling—before you choose to break them. Take a chance. Start submitting your work early and accept that rejection is part of the process. Be open to critique, but never let anyone mess with your vision. Protect the heart of what you're creating.

❱ HISTORICAL MYSTERIES

Arnold, Tedd. *Rat Life*. Sleuth (Penguin Group), 2007.
Winner of the Edgar Award, this 1970s adventure features Todd, a boy who reluctantly helps run his parents' hotel and wants to be a writer. He is drawn

to Rat, a Vietnam War veteran, who helps him find more interesting work. Todd begins to suspect that Rat may be involved with an unsolved murder and tries to piece clues together. Things come to a head when a natural disaster forces them to face each other. (Gr. 7+)

Baratz-Logstead, Lauren. *The Twin's Daughter.* **Bloomsbury, 2010.**
Lucy's pampered life in Victorian London is disrupted when a knock on the door reveals a woman who is the very image of her mother. The woman turns out to be Aunt Helen, the twin raised in poor circumstances while Lucy's mother, Aliese, had privileges. When one of the twins is killed, Lucy is unsure which it was, and she tries to figure it out with the help of attractive neighbor Kit. (Gr. 7+) *See also* Romantic Suspense.

Blundell, Judy. *Strings Attached.* **Scholastic, 2011.**
Kit Corrigan tries to make her way as a dancer in 1950 New York City. One of a set of triplets raised by a single father, she is offered an apartment and a lucrative position by the father of her on-again, off-again boyfriend, Billy, while he is at basic training. Billy's father has mob connections, and he soon is asking Kit for favors. As she tries to pull Billy and herself out of the web of his father's influence, she discovers secrets about her own family. Teens (and adults) may also enjoy the excellent audio version. (Gr. 9+)

Blundell, Judy. *What I Saw and How I Lied.* **Scholastic, 2008.**
In this National Book Award Winner and Edgar-nominated title, Blundell (also known as Jude Watson) brings readers back to 1947. Evie goes to Palm Beach with her parents only to have them enter into a questionable hotel deal with new friends, Arlene and Tom Grayson. Evie begins to fall for the Grayson's friend Peter, then realizes her mother may be involved with him. After a deadly boat accident, Evie's father, Joe, is accused of murder, and she discovers what happened amid the racism and attitudes of the day. (Gr. 9+) *See also* Romantic Suspense.

Bradbury, Jennifer. *Wrapped.* **Atheneum, 2011.**
In Regency England, Agnes Wilkins is bored with her life as a debutante. At the party of her charming adventurer neighbor, she pockets a charm while the guests unwrap the body of a mummy. As the neighbor woos her, she is drawn instead to Egyptologist Caedmon, a working-class man who helps her track down inconsistencies with the artifact. They are further drawn together by danger as a much larger mystery of historical significance unfolds. (Gr. 7+)

Bray, Libba. *The Diviners (The Diviner series).* **Little, Brown, 2012.**
In 1920s New York, readers meet Evie, who enjoys life in the times except for the fact that she has to live with her Uncle Will and help run his occult

museum. When her uncle is called to the scene of a murder of a young girl, Evie realizes her secret gift may help find a killer if she dares to use it. (Gr. 9+) *See also* Fantastic and Paranormal Mysteries—Supersleuths and Special Powers.

Campbell, Eddie. *The Black Diamond Detective Agency.* **First Second, 2007.**
This graphic novel invokes the turn of the twentieth century as it recounts the story of John Hardin, a man on the run. Suspected of being responsible for a devastating Midwest train crash, John evades private detectives and heads to Chicago. Campbell depicts forensic science from that era, including the use of artists. (Gr. 10+)

Chibbaro, Julie. *Deadly.* **Atheneum Books for Young Readers, 2011. (Gr. 7+)**
See High-Tech Whodunits—CSI Teens.

Doyle, Marissa. *Bewitching Season* **(Leland Sisters series). Square Fish, 2009.**
Along with *Betraying Season*, this duet of books features twins Persephone and Penelope as they solve a kidnapping and a treason plot, all the while immersed in the annual social Season. After their beloved governess, Ally, is kidnapped right in Kensington Palace, the twins seek answers. A mix of magic and romance makes these mysteries enjoyable reading as both twins discover that they have the bravery and brains to save everyone. (Gr. 7–10)

Dunlap, Susanne. *The Musician's Daughter.* **Bloomsbury, 2008.**
When the body of her father is returned to 15-year-old Theresa's home on Christmas Eve in eighteenth-century Vienna, her options are limited and immediate. She must find a way to help her pregnant mother and her younger brother, who needs funds to get an apprenticeship. She hopes to play the viola for money rather than marry as her mother hopes. She seeks help from Franz Joseph Haydn, the famous composer, who hires her to clerk for him. She also enlists the help of another man from the orchestra, and they begin to discover what happened to her murdered father. The investigation will pull readers right into this time period, and the plot and characters will make them want to stay. (Gr. 7–10)

Elliott, Patricia. *The Pale Assassin.* **Holiday House, 2009.**
Spoiled Eugenie is aware that the French Revolution is occurring around her, but she is more interested in her social life. Her guardian has secretly promised her hand in marriage to Le Fantome, the Pale Assassin, a hated spy. Eugenie surfaces from parties to combat spies and secrets as she helps her brother, Armand, fight to save the king, working against the Pale Assassin. (Gr. 7–10)

Ford, Michael. *The Poisoned House.* **Albert Whitman, 2011. (Gr. 8+)**
See Fantastic and Paranormal Mysteries—Dark Forces.

Griffin, Adele, and Lisa Brown. *Picture the Dead.* **Sourcebooks Fire, 2010.**
In this richly illustrated story of suspense, Jennie Lovell's twin, Toby, and her fiancé, Will, have been killed in the Civil War. Will's brother, Quinn, returns home a strange man with an unnerving interest in Jennie. She is desperate for a sighting or a message from Will as she tries to protect herself from increasing danger. This unusual, multilayered story is perfect for reluctant readers. (Gr. 7+) *See also* Fantastic and Paranormal Mysteries—Voices from the Beyond. For discussion suggestions, see chapter 6, "When Book Discussions Get Mysterious."

Haines, Kathryn Miller. *The Girl Is Murder* **(The Iris Anderson series). Roaring Brook Press, 2011.**
This Edgar Award–nominated title begins a series about 1942 New York City. Iris wants to help her depressed pop, who has come back from the war missing a leg. Despite his circumstances, he is trying to run his private detective agency, and when one of his cases involves a boy from Iris's school, she starts asking questions. Historical details about the Savoy and other New York City cultural landmarks bring history to life amid an intricate mystery. (Gr. 8+)

Hoffman, Mary. *The Falconer's Knot: A Story of Friars, Flirtation and Foul Play.* **Bloomsbury, 2007.**
In Renaissance Italy, wealthy Silvano, 16, seeks sanctuary with Franciscans after his dagger is found in the body of the husband of his lover, Angelica. As more murders are pinned on him, Silvano discovers another accused teen murderer also hiding in the friary. This well-woven tale of murder, romance, and history will appeal to fans of Hoffman as well as historical fiction. (Gr. 7+) *See also* Romantic Suspense.

Lee, Y. S. *The Agency: A Spy in the House* **(A Mary Quinn Mystery). Candlewick, 2009.**
The first title in this trilogy is the winner of an Agatha Award. Mary is rescued from the gallows at age 12 and brought to a special school to be retrained for polite society. She is then selected to train as a secret agent. Her first assignment is to scrutinize an English family to find the father's connection to pirated goods stolen from India. While investigating, she encounters a clue to the secrets of her own past in this story about a smart, independent woman. (Gr. 7+)

Low, Dene. *Petronella Saves Nearly Everyone: The Entomological Tales of Augustus T. Percival.* **Houghton Mifflin, 2009.**

This 2010 Edgar-nominated title is unusual in that it is set in 1903 England. At Petronella's coming-out party, the heroine's beloved uncle can't stop eating bugs, famous guests are kidnapped, a tent falls on everyone, and her heart races when her best friend Jane's brother, James, is around. When Jane is also kidnapped, Petronella tries to help Scotland Yard with the ransom. Filled with historical detail about everything from S-curve corsets to the novel reading of the day, this madcap caper will delight readers as the smart heroine puts clues together and saves everyone. (Gr. 6–9) *See also* Realistic Mysteries—Humorous Inspectors, or What's So Funny about Crime?

MacLean, Sarah. *The Season.* **Orchard Books, 2009.**

Seventeen-year-old Alexandra is dismayed to find intelligence is not valued as she moves among the balls of the Season. She is attracted to her brother's friend Gavin, who is grieving over his father's death and concerned about his new responsibilities as earl. When she overhears a conversation that unveils the murder of Gavin's father, she decides to solve the mystery. Fun, page-turning reading will attract Regency fans as well as romance fans. (Gr. 7+) *See also* Romantic Suspense.

Riggs, Ransom. *Miss Peregrine's Home for Peculiar Children.* **Quirk Books, 2011. (Gr. 9+)**

See Fantastic and Paranormal Mysteries—Voices from the Beyond.

Sedgwick, Marcus. *Revolver.* **Roaring Brook Press, 2010.**

The 1910 Alaska Gold Rush is the setting for this winner of the 2011 Michael L. Printz Honor Award. Sig and his family know his father should have come home to their cabin after a trip into town. When his father's body is found frozen on the ice, Sig has to stand guard while the others go for help. A mysterious stranger appears and claims that Sig's father owes him money. The man reveals secrets about Sig's father and becomes more threatening by the hour. Sig knows he has to outwit this stranger to save his stepmother and sister, as well as himself. (Gr. 7+)

Silvey, Craig. *Jasper Jones.* **Knopf, 2009.**

Thirteen-year-old Charlie is summoned into the night by school dropout Jasper Jones, who needs Charlie's help covering up a murder. Jasper found the body of his girlfriend, Laura, hanging from a tree and knows he will be blamed. He and Charlie bury her until they can figure out who did this. In the process, Charlie uncovers ugliness in his mining town, from prejudice against his best friend, Vietnamese Jeffrey, to secrets among the town pillars and even to fissures in his own house. Set in 1965 Australia, this Printz Honor Award title is filled with excellent writing and surprises. (Gr. 9+)

For discussion suggestions, see chapter 6, "When Book Discussions Get Mysterious."

Welsh, T. K. *Resurrection Men.* **Dutton, 2007.**
In 1830, Victor is forced to watch the murder of his parents before being sold as a cabin boy. His dark adventures lead him through more sinister forces until he realizes doctors are looking for dead bodies to study, and that industry has become a lucrative black market. Explicit descriptions and themes make this fascinating book a good choice for reluctant older teen readers. (Gr. 10+)

Yancey, Rick. *The Monstrumologist* **(The Monstrumologist series). Simon and Schuster Books for Young Readers, 2010. (Gr. 9+)**
See High-Tech Whodunits—CSI Teens.

ADULT HISTORICAL MYSTERY SERIES FOR TEENS

Hyzy, Julie. *State of the Onion* **(White House Chef Mysteries). Berkley, 2008.**
Ollie keeps the White House kitchen running amid intrigue and protocol in this action-packed series. The themes and programs described in each volume of this award-winning series are steeped in tradition and history. (Gr. 8+)

McCleary, Carol. *The Alchemy of Murder* **(Murder series). Forge, 2010.**
Nellie Bly, the first female investigative reporter, encounters other famous faces from history as she solves cases in this series. As she works on the Jack the Ripper case, she develops a crush on Jules Verne, enjoys conversations with Oscar Wilde, and visits the labs of Louis Pasteur. Each volume in this fun series brings more recognizable faces. (Gr. 9+)

Winspear, Jacqueline. *Maisie Dobbs* **(Maisie Dobbs Mysteries). Penguin, 2004.**
After spending time at Cambridge and working as a nurse in the Great War, Maisie sets up business as a private investigator in the late 1920s. This clever heroine tracks down cases from infidelity to crimes much more dangerous in the popular series. (Gr. 9+)

❱ JAMES BOND AND SHERLOCK HOLMES REVISITED

Re-creating the teen years of famous fictional sleuths is a popular trend. Many authors of adult series are offering teen books featuring their heroes as teens. Here fictional heroes are also given teen years, especially James Bond and Sherlock Holmes.

Higson, Charlie. *SilverFin: A James Bond Adventure* (Young Bond series). Ian Fleming Publications/Hyperion, 2005.

The Young Bond series goes back to James's childhood and his school days at Eton, where he deals with making friends and fighting bullies, but the mysteries are still dark, murderous, and dangerous. In the first title, James learns what happened to a missing boy who was in the wrong place at the wrong time near an eel-infested lake in Scotland. (Gr. 5–8)

Lane, Andrew. *Death Cloud*. (Sherlock Holmes: The Legend Begins series). Farrar, Straus and Giroux, 2010.

Endorsed by the estate of Sir Arthur Conan Doyle, this series shows readers the great detective emerging from an awkward teen. In the first title, Holmes and his tutor, Amyus, find a body, escape from kidnappings, and track a killer. More action than investigative techniques, this series is a good hook for today's teens who are not yet ready for the Doyle stories. (Gr. 7–10)

Scheier, Leah. *Secret Letters*. Hyperion, 2012.

Dora's mother's deathbed confession leads Dora to believe she is the illegitimate daughter of the famous Sherlock Holmes. She travels to London to seek his help with her cousin's ransomed love letters from a secret affair. She arrives on Holmes's doorstep only to learn he has died after plunging off a waterfall. One of his young assistants, Peter, finds her there and is very willing to help her save her cousin. A female heroine with Holmes-type skills may attract even more girls to the Doyle books. (Gr. 8+)

Springer, Nancy. *The Case of the Missing Marquess* (Enola Holmes Mysteries). Philomel, 2006.

Holmes's much-younger sister begins her own series when she determines to discover what happened on her fourteenth birthday when her mother disappeared. She is on the trail of a missing marquess, and readers will be able to solve clues and decipher codes along with her in this well-crafted historical series with exciting modern pacing. (Gr. 5–8)

ADULT SHERLOCK HOLMES REVISITED SERIES FOR TEENS

Horowitz, Anthony. *House of Silk: A Sherlock Holmes Novel* (Sherlock Holmes series). Mulholland Books, 2011.

With approval from the estate of Sir Arthur Conan Doyle, Horowitz brings his skill for action and modern pacing to the voices of Holmes and Watson. This is an attractive bridge series for teens who love Horowitz or Holmes, or both, and are ready for more-adult titles. (Gr. 9+)

▶ YOUNG SLEUTHS FROM POPULAR CONTEMPORARY ADULT SERIES

Coben, Harlan. *Shelter* (A Mickey Bolitar Novel). **Putnam, 2011.**
   Coben began his young adult version of his popular adult series with an Edgar nomination for *Shelter*. Forced to live with his uncle Myron after his father is killed and his mother has to undergo treatment for substance abuse, Mickey encounters weird people in his new town. One woman tells him that his father did not actually die. As he learns more about this woman, he finds himself embroiled in the disappearance of a girl he has met, and the case appears to have historical significance for Mickey. Coben fans will find this title a change of pace, but it is likely to attract new readers. (Gr. 9+)

Parker, Robert B. *Chasing the Bear: A Young Spenser Novel*. **Philomel, 2009.**
   Before his death, Parker published this beginning to a young adult series based on his famous Spenser character, and it is unclear if the series will continue. It is a thrilling page-turner showing a pivotal moment in Spenser's development when he has to do something daring and desperate to save a friend who has been abducted in the West, where Spenser grew up with his father and uncles. (Gr. 8+)

Wilson, F. Paul. *Jack: Secret Histories* (Young Repairman Jack series). **Tor Teen, 2009.**
   In this enjoyable series, Wilson focuses on teenage Jack rather than setting the stage for the future series. Jack and his two friends uncover mysteries in their New Jersey Pine Barrens neighborhood, and Jack's sister dates a law enforcement official, which helps the mystery-solving process. Readers will enjoy learning about the characters in this story as they get sidetracked on interesting tangents, such as investigating the contents of a mysterious box, but otherwise seem normal and realistic. (Gr. 6+)

▶ MYSTERIOUS FLASHBACKS AND TIME TRAVEL

Many stories are pieced together through flashback scenes or time travel. Often the hero or heroine wakes up and does not remember what happened, or the main character receives parts of clues and is led back to discover the rest of the story. This technique is a fun twist on traditional mysteries. This subgenre is similar to the Voices from the Beyond category in the Fantastic and Paranormal Mysteries section and will likely attract those readers, too.

Archer, Jennifer. *Through Her Eyes*. **HarperTeen, 2011.**
   Sixteen-year-old Tansy moves with her mother and ailing grandfather to the town where he grew up. Their house seems to be haunted by the memories

of a troubled teen. Tansy finds a necklace connected to the teen and begins to travel back as his girlfriend, finding not only the teen but her grandfather as well. She becomes absorbed in Henry and her life as Bell. Tate, a modern teen, helps Tansy learn what really happened to Henry and her grandfather while keeping herself safe. (Gr. 8+)

Asher, Jay. *Thirteen Reasons Why*. Razorbill, 2007.
Clay receives a box of cassette tapes from recent suicide victim Hanna. As he listens, he is directed to locations and to stories of what led to her final step. Everyone who received the box is involved with her story. Clay was the lone positive note along Hanna's troubled path, which is slowly pieced together as the story unwinds. The audio version of this story is especially powerful. (Gr. 9+)

Bick, Ilsa. *Draw the Dark*. Carolrhoda, 2010.
After Christian's parents disappear from his Wisconsin town, he goes to live with his Uncle Hank, the local sheriff. Christian keeps his ability to draw and paint others' thoughts and nightmares a secret, but his power is revealed when he realizes he has painted swastikas on a barn. A vision from a man in a nursing home pulls him into decades-long prejudices and murders in the town, and as he tries to sort out those images, he finds himself drawing a new place where he believes his parents have been sent. Older teens will enjoy this compelling and dark tale. (Gr. 9–12)

Gier, Kerstin. *Ruby Red* (Ruby Red series). Henry Holt, 2011.
Gwen's family trained her cousin Charlotte in the family gift of time traveling, but it is Gwen instead who is zapped through time when she turns 16. She encounters a secret society, an attractive yet irritating time-traveling boy named Gideon, and page-turning suspense. (Gr. 6–9) *See also* Fantastic and Paranormal Mysteries—Supersleuths and Special Powers.

Hahn, Mary Downing. *Mister Death's Blue-Eyed Girls*. Clarion, 2012.
Based on an actual event in the author's hometown, this story follows Nora as she tries to learn what happened to two murdered friends in the 1950s. Nora and Ellie let Cheryl and Bobbi Jo go ahead to school when they oversleep. The girls are found murdered—shot—hours later. The townspeople are convinced Cheryl's ex-boyfriend is the killer, but Nora is not sure. As she tries to understand their deaths by thinking back about the dead girls, the ripples from the murder change everything around her. (Gr. 9+)

Henderson, J. A. *Bunker* 10. Harcourt, 2007. (Gr. 7+)
See High-Tech Whodunits—Futuristic Mysteries.

Johnston, Jeffry. *Fragments.* **Simon Pulse, 2007.**

Chase is the only survivor of a car crash, and he can remember only fragments of what happened that night. He had called his ex-girlfriend because he knew she would drive him and two drunk friends home. They were hit by another drunk driver. Chase's father is a busy minister, whose job has required them to move many times. Chase sees his brother Ben, whom no one talks about, in his room and at odd times. A therapist helps Chase deal with OCD and the trauma from the accident and helps him piece together his new reality in this engrossing read. (Gr. 8+)

Larbalestier, Justine. *Liar.* **Bloomsbury, 2009.**

Micah begins the story by telling readers her boyfriend is missing. Then his body is found. Micah tells stories from both the past and the present that show she is a compulsive liar. She also mentions that she used to have a brother. Readers must sort the grains of truth from all the conflicting pieces in this compelling, multilayered psychological mystery. (Gr. 10+)

Lynch, Chris. *Kill Switch.* **Simon and Schuster, 2012.**

Daniel knows his beloved grandfather Da is succumbing to dementia. His stories make less sense, and he has to be watched at all times for his own safety. But Daniel does not understand why Da's old colleagues seem concerned about stories and memories that are surfacing. When plans are made to have Da committed, Daniel helps him escape. Da's stories refer to violence, and Daniel wonders if he ever really knew his grandfather. He learns more about himself, too, in this dark psychological story. (Gr. 9+)

MacCready, Robin Merrow. *Buried.* **Dutton Juvenile, 2006.**

Claudine has spent her life caring for her alcoholic mother. Now her mother is missing, and Claudine is trying to exist without her. Years of abuse and secrets have led Claudine to rock bottom, and readers will keep turning pages to uncover the dark truth she is now hiding behind in this Edgar Award–winning story. (Gr. 9+)

Meldrum, Christina. *Madapple.* **Knopf, 2008.**

Aslaug is on trial for her mother's murder in this layered story about a fringe society. She seems insane, but kernels of truth in her testimony—about having a child and a lover, about being isolated in an apartment—begin to come together. Her mother's religion and love of nature and botany have become twisted in Aslaug's mind. Different points of view contribute to the story until readers will wonder who is really insane. This unique story will inspire sympathy toward Aslaug and her situation as the truth unfolds. (Gr. 9+)

Miller, Barnabas, and Jordan Orlando. *7 Souls.* **Random House Children's Books, 2010.**

This Edgar-nominated title begins when Mary finds herself naked in a department store bed on her seventeenth birthday, with no memories of the night before. Her boyfriend breaks up with her, her mother fights with her, and then she is thrown into the body of each of the people she is closest with. She learns they all hate her for different reasons, and time is running out as she battles a curse. This dark story of paranormal forces sorts through Mary's memories of how she treated those around her. (Gr. 9+) *See also* Fantastic and Paranormal Mysteries—Dark Forces.

Nixon, Joan Lowery. *The Other Side of Dark.* **Delacorte (reprint), 2011.**

Winner of the 1987 Edgar Award, this story will remind readers why Nixon won the Edgar four times. Stacy wakes from a coma after four years, unable to come to terms with her mother's murder and with her new, 17-year-old body. Her mother had been shot as had she, and now she can remember things about the murderer. The news media leak her story, and the murderer now wants her dead, too. She tries to figure out who the killer is before he finds her. (Gr. 7–10)

Price, Charlie. *The Interrogation of Gabriel James.* **Farrar, Straus and Giroux, 2010.**

In this dark, twisted story, 14-year-old Gabriel James tries to explain to police about the two killings he witnessed and what led up to them. Gabriel had pursued a girl and learned of her troubled home life, and it is harder for him to explain his responsibility and involvement after the shocking events unfold. (Gr. 10+)

Reiss, Kathryn. *Blackthorn Winter.* **Harcourt, 2006. (Gr. 8–10)**

See Realistic Mysteries—Small-Town Sleuths.

Summer, Courtney. *Fall for Anything.* **St. Martin's Griffin, 2010.**

After Eddie Reeve's father commits suicide, she is desperate for answers. When she encounters his former photography student Culler Evans, they uncover messages and signs in real life and in their memories, even as her best friend, Milo, refuses to talk to her about that night. Eddie soon begins to doubt what she knows as she is led to terrible truths in this story of psychological suspense. (Gr. 9+)

Tullson, Diane. *Riley Park.* **Orca Soundings, 2009.**
Seventeen-year-old Corbin is known for being a fighter as a hockey player. After he and his friend Darius fight over a girl, they are both attacked at a party. Corbin ends up in the hospital with brain injuries after being hit with a crowbar, and Darius is dead. No one believes Corbin did not kill him. Now Corbin must fight his clouded memory to figure out who did in this fast-paced easy reader. (Gr. 9+)

Warman, Jessica. *Between.* **Walker, 2011. (Gr. 9–12)**
See Fantastic and Paranormal Mysteries—Voices from the Beyond.

▶ COLD CASES AND LOCKED DOORS

Sometimes teen sleuths get involved with riveting cases that seem impossible to solve. Cold cases and locked doors have in common the fact that they seem impenetrable given the current data and set of characters. Savvy sleuths shake loose new angles and information in these puzzles.

Citra, Becky. *Missing.* **Orca, 2011.**
This fast-paced, high-interest/low-level reading title features a cold case and a modern threat. Teen Thea learns about a girl who went missing in the 1950s from the ranch where Thea now lives, and was never found. A local man was arrested, and his grandson now helps Thea look up information about the case. While investigating, they discover a few of their own family secrets and realize that not everyone wants the truth uncovered. (Gr. 6–9)

Dowd, Siobhan. *The London Eye Mystery.* **David Fickling Books, 2008.**
Ted watches his cousin, Salim, go up in a cage of the London Eye, but not come back down. Because Ted, the narrator, has Asperger's syndrome, the clues may not fit in a linear pattern, but readers will be fascinated as Ted and his sister, Kat, begin to piece together what happened to Salim, starting with a camera he left behind. Locked Door mysteries are few and far between, and mystery fans will delight in this one. (Gr. 6+)

McMann, Lisa. *Dead to You.* **Simon Pulse, 2012.**
When Ethan was 7 years old, someone kidnapped him from his yard. At 16 he returns to his family after finding them via a website for missing children. The reintroduction to the family does not go smoothly for everyone, and although Ethan loves his new little sister, Gracie, it is clear that his brother and old friends are conflicted about their feelings for him. Not everyone believes he is Ethan, and readers will be questioning the truth along with the characters. (Gr. 7+)

Plum-Ucci, Carol. *The Night My Sister Went Missing*. Harcourt, 2008.

Kurt and Casey Carmody are not supposed to be at the party on the pier while their parents are out of town. A shot rings out, a splash is heard, and Casey has disappeared. Kurt spends the night at the police station listening to people in the town gossip and accuse Stacy Kearny, who is rumored to be pregnant. This is a taut page-turner with a new twist on the Locked Door mystery. (Gr. 9+)

MYSTERIOUS BOOKTALKING EXAMPLES

The Other Side of Dark by Joan Lowery Nixon

What were you like four years ago? Imagine if you were in a coma and woke up four years from now. What would your friends and family be like? Stacey just woke up. She is now 17, and she can remember things about the shooter who put her in the coma and who murdered her mother. The killer does not want her to remember.

The Night My Sister Went Missing by Carol Plum-Ucci

During a party on a pier a shot rings out, a splash is heard, and Kurt's sister Casey is missing. In this riveting page-turner, Kurt spends a long night listening to conversations at the police station about what everyone thinks they know. Who got shot? Will his sister be saved? Read and find out.

COVERT MARKETING

Attract readers to a display of Sherlock Holmes titles and read-alikes with codes. In "The Adventure of the Dancing Men," Sherlock Holmes cracks the cipher that is illustrated in the story. Give teens a handout that either explains the whole code of the dancing figures or deciphers just a few letters, referencing the story in case they want to read it. Place some signs or a bookmark written in code near a display of mystery books, and invite teens to unravel the code.

ROMANTIC SUSPENSE

Usually, romantic suspense titles are included in other categories, as the romance is merely a fun side aspect of the story rather than the main event of the mystery plot. Readers who like the romantic element will find strong threads of it in these stories.

Interview with APRIL HENRY

After publishing five books for adults, best-selling author April Henry began writing edgy thrillers for young adults. Roald Dahl published her first story, written at age 12. She now alternates between writing for adults and young adults and taking kung fu lessons.

Q: What draws you to the mystery genre?
A: I love reading and writing mysteries and thrillers because they offer the built-in drama of life or death. The stakes can't get any higher. There's also crime fiction for every taste. It can be as cozy or as bloody as you like. The mystery can be solved by cats or shape-shifters, amateurs or professionals.

Life can be pretty random, and real crimes are often senseless. But in a book, you can almost always count on there being a good guy. A good guy who wins at the end. He may be bloody and bruised, but he still wins.

Q: What appealed to you about writing for adults?
A: That's where I originally started. I was reading books for adults because I was one (plus there weren't nearly as many great books for teens as there are now), so when I first started writing, the characters were the same age as me—adults. I had published five books for adults before my first teen book came out. In fact, when I wrote it I thought it was a book for adults that just happened to have a 16-year-old main character. But my agent, who represents a lot of young adult writers, broke the news to me: I had written a YA novel.

Q: How is writing for young adults different?
A: For me, there's not much about the writing that's different. The characters are younger and the books are often shorter, but that's about it. I think everything else that goes on around the two types of books is different, though. Writers of adult books don't have to worry so much about books being challenged. And with teen books, librarians are key to success.

Kids have big emotions about everything, and their feelings about writers are no exception. They will pour out their (sometimes incredibly sad) stories to you, friend you on Facebook (and think you are really friends), hand you poems they wrote and ask what you think, and even ask you to sign their hands. Adults are much more dispassionate.

Q: How did Roald Dahl start your writing career?
A: Writers need an audience. It's not enough to create the story. Without a reader, does it really exist? When I was a kid, Roald Dahl not only wrote the stories I read—he read a story I wrote. I grew up in a small logging town in southern Oregon, where there was little to do if you didn't like to hunt and fish. I practically lived at the Carnegie-funded library. In grade school, I started to write my own stories. One was about a six-foot-tall frog named Herman who loved peanut butter. I decided it would appeal to Roald Dahl, the author of my beloved *Charlie and the Chocolate Factory*. My father had told me that you could write to authors care of their publishers. So I sent off my story—carefully printed in pencil on wide-ruled paper—to the address printed just inside the front cover. And somehow it found its way to Dahl in England. He sent me back a postcard. It's dated 24th August '72, and says, "Dear April, I loved your story about Herman the frog. I read it aloud to my daughter, Ophelia, who also loved it. I read it to my secretary, Hazel, who giggled. Lots of love, Roald Dahl." I've managed to hold onto this postcard for over forty years. It's amazing that he committed this act of kindness for one of what must surely have been a flood of scribbled missives. Dahl even shared the story with the editor of the *Puffin Post*, a British children's magazine. She contacted me and asked to publish it. But even before the magazine came out, I already knew that I was a real writer. Because Roald Dahl had told me so.

Q: Where did you get the idea for Cheyenne in *Girl, Stolen*, and how did you research so you would write from the point of view of a blind person?
A: It was inspired by a story I saw on the local news. A blind girl, Heather Wilson, was with her mom, her mom went into the store and left the keys in the ignition, and someone stole the car. Only in real life she was only in the car for a couple of miles. When she let him know she was there, he let her out. Sure, it was still scary, because she was in the middle of the road in the dark with no idea where she was, but at least she didn't stay kidnapped. When I saw Heather on TV, I immediately knew it would make the great beginning to a book. I read a lot of autobiographies by people who were born blind or went blind, and I interviewed people who were blind, including a girl who was mainstreamed at a high school in Eugene, Oregon. I also talked to an eye doctor about head injuries and blindness. He's the one who told me that a lot of people who go blind as the result of an accident have a tiny, blurry slice of vision left. I spent several hours wandering around my house with my hand over my eyes, trying to figure out how helpful that was. I also went to the Guide Dogs for the Blind school and spent a day there. During the day, they put a blindfold on me and then gave me a dog and a harness and told me to put the latter on the former. That was super hard because I had never seen a harness up close and you have to kind of pull on them to get them to fit snugly. I was worried I might hurt the dog, but I finally got it on. Then I went to pat the dog on the head and realized I had harnessed up the back end!

Q: You portray three-dimensional villains in addition to heroines in both *Girl, Stolen* and *The Night She Disappeared*. Why do you want your readers to see so much of the bad guys, too?
A: I figure I created them, so I should understand how they got to be the kind of people they are. Some I understand completely, like Griffin and his dad, Roy. Others, like the bad guy in *The Night She Disappeared*, I understand less well because I think they are sociopaths. A sociopath is never going to truly see another person as a human being whose feelings matter.

Q: What did you like to read when you were a young adult?
A: I was an insatiable reader. I loved Robert C. O'Brien's *The Silver Crown*. That to me was the perfect book. It had a great twist involving a policeman that I paid homage to in *Girl, Stolen*. I also loved Sylvia Engdahl's *Enchantress from the Stars*. By the time I was 12 or 13, I had read everything in the children's section and ventured upstairs in our library to the adult section. I started with some of the science fiction writers I had known and loved, people like Robert Heinlein and Robert Silverberg. Let's just say that their adult books had a lot more adult content than their books for younger readers, which tend to feature boys in space with slide rules.

Q: What young adult books do you like to read now?
A: I loved Ilsa Bick's *Ashes*, Susan Pfeffer's *Life As We Knew It* (and the follow-up books), Walter Sorrel's *Fake ID*, R. J. Palacio's *Wonder*, Elizabeth Wein's *Code Name Verity*, and Joe Schreiber's *Au Revoir, Crazy European Chick*.

Q: What can schools and libraries do, in your opinion, to connect mysteries to readers?
A: Buy them. Booktalk them. Display them. Advocate for them.

Q: How can adults inspire young people to write?
A: First, give them great books to read, books that they can read at their level, books that speak to them. Writers are first of all readers. Let them be excited by telling a story and don't focus so much on proper grammar, diagramming sentences, finding themes. Let them love the story first.

▶ ROMANTIC SUSPENSE TITLES

Baratz-Logstead, Lauren. *The Twin's Daughter*. Bloomsbury, 2010. (Gr. 7+)
    See Mysteries in Time and Place—Historical Mysteries.

Blundell, Judy. *What I Saw and How I Lied*. Scholastic, 2008. (Gr. 9+)
    See Mysteries in Time and Place—Historical Mysteries.

ADULT ROMANTIC SUSPENSE BOOKS FOR TEENS

Cabot, Meg. *Size 12 Is Not Fat* (Heather Wells series). William Morrow
  Paperbacks, 2005.
Heather is a former pop star whose mother took off with all her earnings. She now
makes her living as an administrator at a college residence hall in New York City.
When one of the residents is killed, Heather wants to know why. Her famous ex-
boyfriend, along with his handsome brother, reenters her life, though she tries to
keep away from her past in this humorous romantic suspense. (Gr. 9+)

Mason, Sarah. *Playing James*. Ballantine Books, 2004.
Holly is desperate for a shot at being a real reporter and agrees to cover the dreaded
crime beat. She is assigned to Sgt. James Sabine, and though they dislike each other
at first, they begin to warm while working through crime stories. A great romance
for teens, as it is a funny British import with chemistry but no sex. (Gr. 8+)

Cusick, Richie Tankersley. *Spirit Walk: Walk of the Spirits and Shadow Mirror*.
  Speak, 2013. (Gr. 8–10)
  See Fantastic and Paranormal Mysteries—Supersleuths and Special Powers.

Derting, Kimberly. *The Body Finder* (The Body Finder Novels series). Harper,
  2010. (Gr. 9+)
  See Fantastic and Paranormal Mysteries—Supersleuths and Special Powers.

Downham, Jenny. *You Against Me*. David Fickling Books, 2011.
  Mikey's sister, Karyn, claims a boy assaulted her at a party, but when Mikey
  goes to the accused's house for a reckoning, he encounters the boy's sister,
  Ellie. She was also at the party, but does not remember all of it. The two of
  them fall for each other as they try to support their families and find out
  what really happened. (Gr. 10–12)

Gerber, Linda. *The Death by Bikini Mysteries* (The Death by . . . Mysteries
  series). Speak (Penguin), 2011. (Gr. 7–10)
  See Realistic Mysteries—Disappearing Friends and Family.

Henry, April. *The Night She Disappeared*. Henry Holt, 2012. (Gr. 8–11)
  See Realistic Mysteries—Disappearing Friends and Family.

Hodkin, Michelle. *The Unbecoming of Mara Dyer* (The Mara Dyer Trilogy).
  Simon and Schuster, 2011. (Gr. 9+)
  See Fantastic and Paranormal Mysteries—Supersleuths and Special Powers.

Hoffman, Mary. *The Falconer's Knot: A Story of Friars, Flirtation and Foul Play*. Bloomsbury, 2007. (Gr. 7+)
See Mysteries in Time and Place—Historical Mysteries.

Ludwig, Elisa. *Pretty Crooked* (Pretty Crooked Trilogy). HarperCollins, 2012. (Gr. 8+)
See Realistic Mysteries—Accused Teens.

MacLean, Sarah. *The Season*. Orchard Books, 2009. (Gr. 7+)
See Mysteries in Time and Place—Historical Mysteries.

Peacock, Kathleen. *Hemlock* (Hemlock series). HarperCollins, 2012. (Gr. 7+)
See Fantastic and Paranormal Mysteries—Creatures with Clues.

MYSTERIOUS BOOKTALKING EXAMPLES

You Against Me by Jenny Downham
Lots of things go on at parties. When Mikey's sister, Karyn, says she was attacked by popular Tom, Mikey goes to Tom's house to confront him the next day. Instead he meets Tom's sister, Ellie, who was at the party but can't remember all of it. Mikey and Ellie begin to like each other while trying to support their families and learn what really happened in this layered romantic suspense.

The Body Finder by Kimberly Derting
Having a special power should be cool, but Violet's talent is discovering the presence of death. She can also sense that a person is a murderer. One day when she is out on a boat, she knows a dead teen is under the water. She does not even want to tell her best friend, Jay, about her skill, even as he knows she is getting involved in finding out who killed the girl. Her feelings for Jay are complicated enough. For teens who enjoy crime, the supernatural, and romance, this series makes great reading.

COVERT MARKETING

To accompany a display of romantic suspense titles, cut magnetized craft sheets into puzzle pieces and leave them near the books for teens to put together. The pieces could form a heart when put together. Or put a drawing of a heart cut into puzzle pieces on bookmarks featuring romantic suspense titles.

Chapter Three

NONFICTION
AND TRUE CRIME

F
or teens who enjoy nonfiction, real-life mysteries are
abundant. The increasing number of television shows that
feature forensic science has fueled an interest in the evidence from both cold cases and current crimes. Ann Rule
remains popular for her true crime titles, though much
of her work covers crimes with mature themes, so finding titles for
younger teens is challenging. Nonfiction books on the Navajo code
talkers, ciphers, and forensics may appeal to younger teens.

The Association for Library Service to Children awards the
Robert F. Sibert Informational Book Medal annually along with
Honor titles. The Young Adult Library Services Association presents
an annual Excellence in Nonfiction Award with four Honor titles.
YALSA also gives its Alex Awards for adult fiction and nonfiction
titles that are excellent for teens. These are all good sources for nonfiction on crime and mystery topics. Many recent titles are geared
toward teens and make for excellent classroom projects as well as
pleasure reading.

Interview with MARC ARONSON

Author and editor Marc Aronson brings a love of young adult literature and a PhD in history to his writing. A long proponent of
nonfiction geared toward teens, Aronson tackles topics and primary
sources in an appealing, thought-provoking fashion. *Sugar Changed
the World* . . . by Aronson and his wife, Marina Budhos, was a finalist
for the YALSA Nonfiction Award. In 2000, Aronson won the first
Sibert Medal for his title *Sir Walter Raleigh and the Quest for El*

Dorado. In *Master of Deceit,* Aronson looks at an interesting period of history during which the FBI was possibly motivated more by politics than by mission.

Q: Why are teens drawn to reading nonfiction about crime, especially with well-known people, as in *Master of Deceit*?

A: Crime has many different kinds of appeal—it can be scary, gory, terminal without being directly threatening, and it is a mystery. When you add in the element of a real person who is famous in other ways—politics, national stature, wealth, and the like—you add in new elements. There is a natural desire to bring down the icon, to get the inside scoop, the real story, and to expose some hidden side most people do not know. In all mystery there is always the desire to outsmart others and to be a hero—to see what others fail to notice and in that way to master the situation. Finally I wonder if teenagers are living a mystery—confusions about their own identity, relationships with peers, with parents, about the future; having a greater need to cover up things they don't want known, and also a desire to be good and to expose secrets held by parents and other adults. So a clear-cut mystery a reader can resolve restores some order to an otherwise perplexing life.

Q: What drew you to write it? What are you hoping teens will take from this book?

A: I had two motivations—one, to explain a man central to America for half of the twentieth century, and two, to use him to challenge (and invite) teenagers to think about security, privacy, and danger today. I also found Hoover himself engagingly dark and mysterious. I wanted to figure him out, to make sense of him.

Q: I enjoyed your chapter on how you did the research. What part of the research for this book surprised you?

A: Surprises? I did not know the rumors about Hoover and passing before I began my research, so that was new. Related to that, I think I was most pleased by the photo research I did in the National Archives. I saw images that seemed to fit with Hoover's racial ambiguity (he is very, very dark at times); I found images of his home that seemed to fit a man at war with his own sexuality. All of these images opened doors to speculation, which I was eager to share with readers—and was able to do in the various dossiers in the book.

Q: Could or do, in your opinion, secrets occur like this today?

A: In some ways today is worse because those eager to gather our personal secrets are not just rogue government agencies but very wealthy corporations tracking our digital lives. I think government is more responsible today and is watched more closely. But the tension between our liberties as individuals and the government's eagerness to have access to more and more about us in order to protect us remains real.

Q: What did you like to read as a teen? What do you find exciting about nonfiction for teens today?
I loved reading nonfiction—*Aku-Aku* by Thor Heyerdahl (his theories about Easter Island); *Kon-Tiki* (his effort to sail there in a reed boat to prove his theory)—but I also loved the U.S.A. Trilogy by John Dos Passos—novels in a very lively and experimental style that anticipated crawlers and tweets—about the first quarter of the twentieth century.

❯ NONFICTION AND TRUE CRIME TITLES

Alphin, Elaine Marie. *An Unspeakable Crime: The Prosecution and Persecution of Leo Frank.* Carolrhoda, 2010.
 The notable mystery fiction writer accomplishes gripping nonfiction as well with this study of the 1913 murder of Mary Phagan and the subsequent punishment the local community handed down on Leo Frank. Frank's life was tarnished by this crime and his arrest for it. He was finally pardoned in 1986, many decades after his death. Alphin collected anecdotal evidence and original papers to document this compelling book. (Gr. 9+) For discussion suggestions, see chapter 6, "When Book Discussions Get Mysterious."

Aronson, Marc. *Master of Deceit: J. Edgar Hoover and America in the Age of Lies.* Candlewick, 2012.
 When Martin Luther King Jr. received an anonymous letter, he believed someone was attempting to blackmail him into committing suicide. Aronson makes a credible case that the author of the letter may have been assistant FBI director William Sullivan, who was following J. Edgar Hoover's principles. Fascinating sources provide interesting and thought-provoking reading. Aronson includes a chapter on how he researched this topic. (Gr. 9+) For discussion suggestions, see chapter 6, "When Book Discussions Get Mysterious."

Bartoletti, Susan. *They Called Themselves the K.K.K.* Houghton Mifflin, 2010.
 Award-winning Bartoletti sets the stage for readers by recounting the history of the time leading up to the creation of the infamous organization. She adds interesting details about how the K.K.K. got its name and original rules and includes startling drawings and photographs from the Library of Congress and other sources. Also fascinating are the time line and source notes detailing the thousands of pages the author studied to bring this difficult subject into a readable, engrossing form. (Gr. 9+)

Barton, Chris. *Can I See Your ID? True Stories of False Identities*. Dial, 2011.
Ten stories of extreme identity theft portrayed in true crime style and with riveting illustrations bring readers into the minds of the criminals. (Gr. 7+)

Blumenthal, Karen. *Bootleg: Murder, Moonshine, and the Lawless Years of Prohibition*. Flash Point/Roaring Brook Press, 2011.
This YALSA Excellence in Nonfiction Honor Award title shows the far-reaching effects of Prohibition. Stories featuring bootlegging, describing how even children were involved, make for fascinating reading and discussion. Did a law that did not make sense cause people to become criminals? (Gr. 8+)

Bowers, Rick. *Spies of Mississippi: The True Story of the Spy Network That Tried to Destroy the Civil Rights Movement*. National Geographic Society, 2010.
Although many know about the K.K.K. and the terrible beatings and murders during the civil rights movement, the spy network is less well known. Teens will be amazed by the primary source material Bowers used to shine a light on this shameful aspect of U.S. history. (Gr. 9+)

Cullen, Dave. *Columbine*. Twelve, 2009.
Cullen spent over a decade studying the evidence and testimony from one of the worst school mass murders in U.S. history. He demolishes rumors and common stories about the killers and victims to portray a chilling scene. (Gr. 9+)

Janeczko, Paul. *The Dark Game: True Spy Stories*. Candlewick, 2010.
Janeczko brings readers a history of the spy industry from the Revolutionary War to recent decades. He also recounts famous missions, including the work of the Choctaw code talkers during World War I and the clandestine efforts of Soviet operatives, in this YALSA Nonfiction Award finalist. (Gr. 8+)

Sheinkin, Steve. *The Notorious Benedict Arnold: A True Story of Adventure, Heroism, and Treachery*. Flash Point/Roaring Brook Press, 2011.
Readers will have been briefly exposed to Arnold's history in class, but this book brings his career and actions into vivid focus. Arnold was not all evil traitor, and teens viewing the primary source material can ponder the famous character in this 2012 YALSA Nonfiction Award winner. (Gr. 8+)

MYSTERIOUS BOOKTALKING EXAMPLES

Can I See Your ID? by Chris Barton
What is identity theft? How does it happen? Who does it? Get into the minds of these tenacious criminals as they take over lives and cause mayhem.

Master of Deceit by Marc Aronson
What is the mission of the FBI? Who do operatives and leaders report to? Would you believe an FBI high-ranking official sent a letter threatening Martin Luther King Jr.? Why would a president endorse a crime? Aronson will lead you through a time when one of our country's greatest crime-fighting organizations was led astray.

COVERT MARKETING

Cut up fake library cards so that they are still somewhat recognizable and scatter them around a copy of *Can I See Your ID?* by Chris Barton (or a poster showing the cover of the book) or copies of books with Internet safety themes. On a poster or handout, print tips on protecting teens' identities online.

PART II
MYSTERIOUS PROGRAMS FOR TEENS

Chapter Four

USING CLUES TO MATCH TEEN INTERESTS
MYSTERIOUS PROGRAMMING

E ven armed with a list of books for teen mystery fans, library staff will still need to connect those books to readers. The following chapters cover many aspects of programming and promotion of mystery titles. Topics include mystery programs, a mystery dinner script, activities for a teen mystery club (see also chapter 5), and suggestions for marketing. Ideas presented in this section may appeal to a wider range of teen patrons than just mystery fans, though they will be especially enjoyed by that group.

This chapter features ten complete program ideas, from preparation through execution. The final program is a full mystery dinner, including an interactive script for improvisational actors. Online program options are included, and variations for cost considerations are suggested. For example, the mystery dinner could have snacks or an ice cream sundae bar rather than pizza.

GET A CLUE: A MYSTERY-THEMED READING PROGRAM

Have teens plan a winter reading program or a year-round reading program with a mystery theme. The program does not have to be restricted to mystery reading, which may turn off some potential readers, but it should celebrate that genre and include some matching activities.

LENGTH OF PROGRAM	NUMBER OF TEENS	GRADE RANGE
6 weeks to 3 months for a winter reading program, or 9 months for a school-year reading incentive program	Unlimited	Grades 5–12

SHOPPING LIST
- Prizes for reading program milestones
- Prizes for solving the crime

SET IT UP
THREE MONTHS BEFORE
- Invite your teen advisory board or Mind-Bending Mystery Club members to design a fictional crime, such as a theft or a kidnapping, with nine to twelve clues. The teens should create a basic description or drawing of a crime scene, with sketches of several of the characters involved. Construct and photograph a sample crime scene with props in the library. Either leave the scene up to advertise the program or set it up again a couple of weeks before the program begins. Prepare posters advertising the upcoming reading program with the drawing of the crime scene or a description of the crime.

TWO WEEKS BEFORE
- Purchase prizes for teens who complete the required number of books for the program as well as for those who solve the crime. Another option is to have a raffle for those who solve the crime.

MAKE IT HAPPEN
Teens will receive a dossier, or a basic description of the crime and characters, along with their book log. These could be available online as well. As they finish each book or two, they will receive a clue. Another option is to reveal a clue every week or two throughout the event on a website or through social media. Readers can turn in a solution to the crime at any time and continue reading.

CRAFTY CLUES

Let teens create with several mediums in this interactive event. It is also a great way to clean out the closet!

LENGTH OF PROGRAM	NUMBER OF TEENS	GRADE RANGE
1 hour	20 to 25	Grades 5–9

SHOPPING LIST
- Basic crafting supplies such as fabric and craft glue, scissors, markers, duct tape, table coverings
- Scraps of paper, fabric, glitter/sequins, pom-poms, and the like work best with this event

SET IT UP
ONE MONTH BEFORE
- Begin collecting interesting leftover craft supplies from previous programs. Ask staff to recycle boxes of varying sizes to donate for this event.

ONE HOUR BEFORE
- Put an assortment of the craft materials on each covered table where teens will be sitting.

MAKE IT HAPPEN
Invite teens to sit at tables. Some of these activities could be done in teams, or if there are few craft supplies, invite the teens to work in groups. For the first activity, ask them to design something to wear from the items on the table. To tie this program in to the mystery theme, they could design an item of clothing useful for a disguise or for spying. Give them fifteen minutes, then allow five minutes for sharing.

For the second activity, set up teams and ask each team to design something they could use in school or on a fictional spy mission. Again, allow fifteen minutes for creation. Use the remaining five minutes for teens to guess what the other teams' projects are. The team that correctly guesses the most items wins.

For the last activity, invite teens to design a carrier or container and decorate it using a seasonal or book-related or mystery theme. Again, allow fifteen minutes for creation and five for sharing.

SPIES GO GREEN: ELECTRONICS RECYCLING DRIVE

Consider hosting a recycle drive for small or handheld electronics while spy books are on display, and put the collection container near the display of books. Use a simple code to encrypt the words "Spy Stories" and put the code on a sign near the books.

LENGTH OF PROGRAM	NUMBER OF TEENS	GRADE RANGE
1 month	Unlimited	Grades 5+

SHOPPING LIST
- Containers or boxes to collect materials
- Art supplies to decorate the containers
- Prizes for raffle winners

SET IT UP
THREE MONTHS BEFORE
- Find out what types of small electronics or print cartridges can be collected in your community or state. Staff may want to contact local government offices to see what can be collected and how items can be delivered to recycling centers.

ONE MONTH BEFORE
- Make posters and signs (with photos, if possible) of the types of items that can be collected. Prepare a display of fiction and nonfiction books and media on spies. Invite teens to decorate the boxes or collection containers for different items, such as print cartridges or handheld electronics. Make a flier with a line in code along with facts on electronics, recycling, and the environment. At the bottom of the flier, include a form that people can fill out to enter a drawing when they turn in items or solve the code. Award a prize or offer a green incentive, such as clearing fines or allowing extra library checkouts. Make a drop box for drawing entries at the site of the display.

MAKE IT HAPPEN
Set up the display and containers. Check the raffle drop box and empty the containers frequently. Members of the Mind-Bending Mystery Club or other teen volunteers may offer to deliver the items to the recycling center.

CLASSIC MYSTERY MOVIE SERIES

Encourage love of the genre by showing some classic mystery movies to teens.

LENGTH OF PROGRAM	NUMBER OF TEENS	GRADE RANGE
2–2.5 hours	25 if discussion after the movie is desired; otherwise unlimited	Grades 8+

SHOPPING LIST
- Popcorn or snacks (optional)

SET IT UP
THREE MONTHS BEFORE
- Advertise the program or series with movie posters featuring the title. Arrange copies of the book or a display of teen mysteries to match the film.

ONE HOUR BEFORE
- Set up snacks and movie.

MAKE IT HAPPEN
Show classic mystery movies such as *Murder on the Orient Express* or Hitchcock movies such as *The 39 Steps*. Introduce the movie by telling the teens when it was made and mentioning any interesting trivia and any books that may be related.

After the movie, invite teens to participate in a discussion about the ending, or poll the audience about other movies they might want to watch. To build interest in your movie program, conduct an online poll in which teens nominate and then vote on the worst mystery ending they have ever read or viewed. Schools or libraries with less time may choose to show episodes from the *Veronica Mars* television series or the several different TV versions of *Sherlock Holmes* instead of a feature film.

WHAT HAPPENS NEXT?

This activity can be adapted to any genre or even to graphic novels. It is also an easy event to put online. Invite members from the writing club, teen advisory board, or Mind-Bending Mystery Club to create an intriguing beginning to a story. Then let teens take it away!

LENGTH OF PROGRAM	NUMBER OF TEENS	GRADE RANGE
1 week each month, or occasional program	Unlimited	Grades 6–12

SHOPPING LIST
• Small prizes, if this is a raffle event

SET IT UP
THREE MONTHS BEFORE
• Begin promoting the activity through the library's online and in-person marketing channels. Invite teen mystery club members to help create the opening paragraph or page. If this is an ongoing event, provide a new beginning each month and have monthly raffle drawings for teens who participate.

DAY OF PROGRAM
• Post the opening section and activate the comments feature so teens can add to the story. It may be a good idea to set up a filter so comments are reviewed by staff before they are displayed.

MAKE IT HAPPEN
When this program works best, teens will send in sentences about what happens next in the stories and keep adding to each other's entries. To keep the momentum going, post a recurring storyline each month or a themed tie-in and make previous months' entries accessible for teens to read.

DESIGN A GADGET CONTEST

Another great mystery- or spy-themed program is a Design a Gadget Contest. This event can also be adapted to mystery-related themes or planned for older or younger teens with variations (listed in the Make It Happen section).

LENGTH OF PROGRAM	NUMBER OF TEENS	GRADE RANGE
1 week	Unlimited	Grades 6+

SHOPPING LIST
- Prizes
- Miscellaneous supplies for some of the variations

SET IT UP
THREE MONTHS BEFORE
- Make entry forms that include space for drawing a gadget and an area to describe its use. Ask teens to explain how their gadget would make life easier for a detective or a spy.

AFTER THE EVENT
- Invite teen mystery club members to judge the entries. Choose categories such as Most Creative, Best Drawing, and so on, allowing for more winners if there are many entries. Post the winning entries online or display them on posters near theme-related books and media.

MAKE IT HAPPEN: VARIATIONS
LEGOS OR TINKERTOYS
- This program could be an in-library event or a good makerspace activity. Many schools have competitions with Lego robots and similar projects, and this may be a simpler approach that would invite younger teens or more teens to participate. As in the Crafty Clues program described earlier in this chapter, provide a variety of building materials and give the teens a limited amount of time to create a themed device, such as a spying gadget or a crime-solving tool. (This activity can easily be adapted to many themes, and potential devices are unlimited, such as items to do chores, help with pets, or make life easier in general.)

COMPUTER ANIMATION
- Offer a workshop or tutorial on a simple animation program such as Pencil and have a contest for teens to create a working spy gadget in that format. Running videos on your teen website may invite entries or provide publicity for future events.

TRUE OR FALSE? EVERYDAY MYSTERIES

Is truth stranger than fiction? Use popular mystery themes to do a live or online trivia game with teens. This program can also help you highlight your library's reference databases.

LENGTH OF PROGRAM	NUMBER OF TEENS	GRADE RANGE
1 hour	24 teens in teams of four maximum	Grades 7–10

SHOPPING LIST
• Prizes

SET IT UP
THREE MONTHS BEFORE
• The most labor-intensive part of this program is researching the questions and answers. Consider having Mind-Bending Mystery Club members or other teen groups help with this. Now is also a good time to step up promotion of the event through schools and online library venues.

ONE WEEK BEFORE
• Using construction paper and posterboard, construct a simple *Jeopardy*-style board with questions and point values, or plan on taping them to a write-on board. There are likely computerized ways to do this as well, though staff will have to unveil the questions and total points quickly.

DAY OF PROGRAM
• Set up the game and laptops for teams. If the program will feature the library databases, each laptop should be set to the access page.

MAKE IT HAPPEN
Invite teens to group themselves into teams of four, and draw to see which team goes first. Let teens choose categories and point values as in *Jeopardy*. Categories could include mystery book authors or characters, or children's mystery series topics. Other mystery theme categories could be forensic terms, gadgets, or local laws. You might match questions to your library's reference databases and let teens look up answers.

For an online version of this program, post a few questions and award points to the teen who first answers correctly. This activity is a good way to show teens what databases and reference materials they can access from home.

IDENTIFY THE MYSTERIOUS GADGET

Have you cleaned the library's basement lately? Are there any old media formats or players lurking? Consider using old gadgets for a new program!

LENGTH OF PROGRAM	NUMBER OF TEENS	GRADE RANGE
Weekly online event	Unlimited	Grades 6+

SHOPPING LIST
• Prizes

SET IT UP
ONE WEEK BEFORE
• This program is easy to plan and prepare. Find an unusual piece of library equipment—the older, the better. Take a picture of it and post the picture online.

MAKE IT HAPPEN
Invite teens to identify the gadget and its use. Teen responses should go to staff members rather than be posted publicly unless the point of the program is to inspire creativity. Award prizes for Best Answer or Most Creative as judged by teen mystery club members.

PUZZLING PROGRAM

Who knew putting puzzles together could be extreme? This puzzle-building program can be offered as a drop-in activity or as a competition.

LENGTH OF PROGRAM	NUMBER OF TEENS	GRADE RANGE
1 hour	24 or unlimited with drop-in variation	Grades 6+

SHOPPING LIST
- Four copies (if possible) of the same 500-piece puzzle for competition
- Several types of puzzles, including Jenga, Rubik's Cube, or vintage items, and puzzles with varying numbers of pieces for drop-in program
- Timer
- Prizes for competition

SET IT UP
ONE MONTH BEFORE
- Prepare signs with big lettering advertising the event. Cut the signs into pieces and post a few pieces at a time in the teen area to catch attention. Make sure the complete puzzle is up at least a week before the event so people know when to come!

ONE HOUR BEFORE
- Set up tables with chairs around puzzles.

MAKE IT HAPPEN
If this program is going to be a competition, invite teens to sit in teams around tables with the same puzzle on each. The team that finishes first wins. Award a prize for the winning team.

If the program is a drop-in activity, create stations with different types of puzzles. For example, one station may have word puzzles, another may have Jenga, a third may have a traditional jigsaw puzzle, and a fourth may be a make-your-own puzzle (include a die-cutter). Mix things up by setting the timer to go off every ten or fifteen minutes and have teens switch stations.

Mystery Puzzle Variation: Another alternative is to have teams put together puzzles without a photo to work from.

TEEN MYSTERY DINNER SCRIPT: WHO KILLED IMA GUDEATER?

This is an outline and script for a simple teen mystery dinner with a library setting. The event should require only one rehearsal. Plan on serving snacks or dessert while cast members circulate and answer last-minute questions from the audience while the teams decide on their killer.

LENGTH OF PROGRAM	NUMBER OF TEENS	GRADE RANGE
60 minutes	50, plus 10 cast members	Grades 7–12

SHOPPING LIST
- Drinks
- Pizza
- Snacks or dessert (to be served at breaks during the event or instead of pizza)
- Paper goods for serving
- Props for mystery (see Make It Happen)
- Costumes and props for each character (for example, a badge, a notebook, and a pen for the detective)
- Prizes for the winning team and for the most creative team, possibly mystery books

SET IT UP
ONE MONTH BEFORE
- Recruit teen volunteers and match them to parts. Most parts can be played by either a male or female, with some adjustment. Send cast members their profile and the questions they will be asked, along with the time line for the evening. With a younger cast, it may be best to have a willing local detective or other adult be the interrogator, as that is a big part. Alternatively, have two detectives and let them split the questioning.
- Make a handout for the audience that includes a brief description of each character and a time line, along with space for notes.
- Create forms for teens to turn in—one per table—showing who was the murderer and why.

TWO WEEKS BEFORE
- Go over the entire program with the cast. Some may need to review their interrogation a few times.
- Shop for needed supplies and paper goods for serving food at the program.

DAY OF PROGRAM
- Set up the room.
- The cast should be in place a half hour before the program begins.
- Order pizza or set up other food options.

MAKE IT HAPPEN
CHARACTERS
- Detective
- Steve Livin
- Ken Livin
- Dynamite Debby
- Penny Pincher
- Bud Reddiholp
- Katie Shy
- Ned Notwork
- Priscilla Vampiran
- Olga Ivanajob

PROPS
- Sign for door indicating that the room is the Twilight Public Library
- Crime scene tape decorating door, room
- Tables and chairs for audience set up in the room
- Table at the front of the room for interrogation
- Table for food and beverages

SETUP
- The Detective checks audience members' names off a list as they come in, asking such questions as "What's your business here?" or "Haven't I seen you before?"
- Audience members sit in teams at tables. At each table is a cast member talking in character about the library and the training. Cast members should be fuming that they are being kept for the investigation.
- Pizza is laid out on a table, and audience members can help themselves after finding their seats.

ACTION
- The Detective calls the room to order and deputizes everyone present to help him solve the crime. He will then go over the following time line, which is also in the handout.
- The Twilight Public Library (TPL) staff began their annual training day on Saturday, June 24, at 9:00 a.m. The Livin brothers spoke and sold their book until 10:30 a.m. Dynamite Debby spoke from 10:30 to 11:30 a.m. Beginning at 10:45, staff on the training day committee set up for lunch, scheduled for 11:30. At 11:45, two staff members, Ima Gudeater and Ned Notwork, ate the salad (the only two staff members to do so). Ima turned purple and gasped for breath. She then fell to the floor and almost instantly died. She was heard saying, "Peanuts." Ned Notwork threw up at 12:45 and was taken to a local hospital, where he was given Benadryl for mild allergy to strawberries and released, unharmed. After Ima died, an anonymous call was made to the police,

who arrived at 12:15. They did a preliminary interview of all people present and retained them for further questioning as "persons of interest."

- The Detective will then call the characters to the table for questioning. When questioning is finished, the audience members may have dessert or snacks while cast members circulate, answering last-minute questions in character. The first team to turn in their sheet with the correct answers wins.

INTERROGATION INFORMATION

The following information should be given to all the cast members ahead of time for rehearsal. It contains everything they need to know for their characters as well as the questions to be asked by the Detective during the show. The audience will get brief descriptions on their own handout with enough information to follow along but not enough to give away the plot.

The Livin Brothers: Hosts of a nationally syndicated late-afternoon talk show, *Livin' It Up.* They have published several books and are hired across the country for inspirational speaking. They speak with a slight twang and refer to their hardscrabble roots and how they "pulled themselves up by their bootstraps," but they are actually from Elmhurst, a wealthy Chicago suburb. Recent publicity has lessened the show's popularity. Ima grew up in Elmhurst as well and went to school with the brothers.

Steve "Steady" Livin: A speaker on money. He has a 13-year-old son, Hardy Livin, whom he adopted shortly after high school. The child is in fact Ken and Ima's, and Steve adopted the boy. Ima had no interest in the child. Steve thinks that healthy eating and purification are a lot of hogwash, but as long as they continue to sell books, he goes along with it. He focused his part of the Twilight Library presentation on "Livin' it up within your means," though his annual salary is over $5 million. He owns thirty credit cards and has a private accountant take care of his money—both little-known secrets. Several websites pay homage to him and his financial genius, so he must maintain the façade. He arrived at 7:45 a.m. on the day of the program, with Ken.

Name:

Occupation: Relationship to Ima:

Did you know her before this training?

What is your son's name?

How old is he?   Isn't he adopted?

Who are his biological parents?

Are you and your brother close?

What was your presentation about?

How much did you earn last year?

I have credit reports that show several credit cards. How many do you have?

You and your brother preach about healthy living. Do you live by that rule?

When did you arrive today?

Did you see anyone else?

Ken "Clean" Livin: A health and lifestyle guru. Although he touts healthy cooking and yoga, he smokes and drinks on the sly. He receives more requests for personal appearances than his brother. He has been getting back together with high school girlfriend Ima quietly and is thinking about telling his adopted nephew, Hardy, who his biological parents are. Steve does not want this to ever happen. Steve does not trust that the relationship with Ima will last and thinks it will damage Hardy. Ken has a reputation for being a ladies' man and has dated Taylor Swift. He arrived at 7:45 a.m. on the day of the program, with Steve.

Name:

Occupation:	Relationship to Ima:

Did you know Ima previous to today?

So she was your girlfriend?	Did you date Taylor Swift?

Are you and your brother close?	Are you close with your nephew?

So he's really your biological son?	Does he know that?

When did you arrive today?

Did you see anyone else?

Dynamite Debby: A landscaping guru. Penny Pincher asked her to speak about DIY gardening, as TPL is soon going to ask staff to maintain the grounds of the library to save money. No one knows Dynamite's real name, or her background, but rumors of time spent in Special Military Explosives Divisions abound. She does use some unusual methods to permanently rid properties of rodents, but she skillfully covers up holes with creative and decorative techniques. She has a PhD in chemistry and has written volumes on fertilizer. Two years ago it was rumored that someone was badly hurt when she re-landscaped a golf course, but the terms of that settlement are permanently sealed. The staff is very unhappy about having to do landscaping, and Debby actually received a threat before the training day. Police found two bowie knives and a small pistol on her person after Ima died. She maintains that they are necessary for gardening.

Name:

Occupation: Relationship to Ima:

We couldn't find much on you. What did you do in the military?

What is your degree in?

What happened when you landscaped our local golf course?

We found several weapons on you today.
Why were you carrying those to a library training?

Did you want Ima dead?   Did you kill her by accident?

Penny Pincher: The staff accountant. Penny is the first accountant in the library's history to turn a bad deficit around and actually make a profit in some areas. Although she is somewhat liked by the staff for not cutting their salaries, they resent the cleaning and landscaping that she is now asking them to do. It is rumored that she tried to blackmail some staff members to raise more money, using secrets from the personnel files. Patrons have not been happy with the increases in fines and the aggressive collection department Penny developed. When the coffee machine disappeared, her 2010 Porsche was keyed in the parking lot. Ima purchased a new coffeemaker with her own money the next day. Penny came in at 7:15 to "help" with the training preparations.

Name:	
Occupation:	Relationship to Ima:
Did you and Ima get along?	
What happened to your car?	
Why doesn't the staff like you?	
When did you come in today?	Did you see anyone?

Bud Reddiholp: A former library maintenance man who is helping TPL with projects to fulfill his 360-hour community service requirement. This punishment was a result of his fraud conviction for selling another library's property on eBay. Bud is well liked by staff and diligent in his work. It has been noticed that he empties the garbage in the business office and at Ned's workstation ten to fifteen times a day, and he has been seen dumping some of the papers into his car. After Ima's death, he admitted that he heard Ima and Penny shouting on several occasions, usually about "cuts to pensions." He was first in line to get an autographed book from the Livin brothers. He also admitted that he saw Penny rifling through the personnel records the day before the training. She said she was double-checking the ages of employees who had been denied retirement privileges for being too young at 75. He came in at 5:30 a.m. and chatted with Katie off and on in the kitchen.

Name:	
Occupation:	Relationship to Ima:

Did everyone get along with Ima?

Why don't you think so?

Why are you doing community service here again?

What do you do here?

How often do you empty the trash?

Do you put it all in the recycling or the dumpster? Why not?

Did you see anything mysterious lately?

What time did you get in today?   Did you see anyone?

Katie Shy: Teen services librarian. She was responsible for the food for the training day. Although Katie maintains a calm demeanor in the midst of any teen program, occasionally she will lose her temper and shout cuss words at anyone passing by, especially if she hasn't had any caffeine. It does take a great deal to get her to this point—such as someone participating in risky health behavior or possibly removing the coffeemaker. She prepared the sandwiches, side dishes, salads, and desserts for the training herself, starting at 5:30 a.m., as Penny would not allow the staff to hire a caterer. She left the kitchen area at 7:00 to go get lattes for herself and Ima from a local coffee shop. She returned at 7:20. At 7:30 a.m., Ned heard her cussing Ima, who had spilled both coffees.

Name:

Occupation: Relationship to Ima:

What time did you arrive?   Did you see anyone else?

Did you get along with Ima?   Did you ever disagree with her?

When did you come in today?   Did you see anyone?

Did you lose your temper today and kill her?

Ned Notwork: IT manager and reference librarian at TPL. He works generally from 7:00 a.m. until midnight, maintaining that this schedule is necessary to keep up the network, though Penny complains about the use of electricity. FBI agents came to TPL last week and met with Ned and Director Vampiran for five hours. After that, the computer network was down for four hours, and Ned took three days off. He returned the day before the training. Ned avoids staff functions, such as the training, like the plague and works as few hours as possible at the reference desk. Patrons often are unable to understand his mumbling. He arrived at the training at 7:30 a.m. and offered to help Katie set up the food. He is mildly allergic to strawberries and ate part of one by accident in the salad. He is a vegetarian.

Name:

Occupation: Relationship to Ima:

Why were you questioned by the FBI?

Why do you work such long hours?

What time did you arrive today?

Did you see anyone else?

Priscilla Vampiran: Head of the Twilight Public Library. She has worked with Ima for many years. They get along, but Ima made no secret of the fact that she wanted the director's job before Priscilla was hired. Priscilla is 30, the youngest director in the history of TPL. She likes to wear stylish, youthful clothing, and Ima felt that the men on staff liked her too much. Ima had been known to act first and then tell Priscilla when she knew that the director wouldn't approve. For example, Ima contacted the FBI about Ned Notwork before letting Priscilla know what was going on. The two had an argument over this, and Ima agreed to suspend Ned rather than fire him outright pending police action and his improved work attitude. Priscilla came in at 7:30 a.m. the morning of the in-service with a box of bagels, as she thought that the staff should have a treat and that Penny was being too cheap about the whole thing. She met Olga in the parking lot and walked her to her locker to collect her belongings. She escorted Olga out at 7:45 a.m.

Name:

Occupation: Relationship to Ima:

Did you and Ima get along?   Why not?

What time did you come in today?   What did you do then?

Olga Ivanajob: Checkout clerk at the library until yesterday, when she was fired by Ima Gudeater. She is 72 years old and argued often with Penny, as she wanted to retire. After yesterday's argument, Ima heard her mutter under her breath that she wanted to poison Penny's lunch. Olga is well known on the staff for bringing in delicious treats, but once someone became ill from a cheesecake that sat out too long in the staff lounge. She supports nineteen grandchildren on her salary and was upset over being fired. She desperately wants her job back. She came in at 7:30 to clean out her locker and meet Director Vampiran to beg for her job. She stopped only to go to the washroom and left the library at 7:45 a.m.

Name:

Occupation: Relationship to Ima:

Did you and Ima get along?

Why were you fired?

Were you mad about that?   Enough to kill?

What time did you come in?   What did you do then?

AFTER THE INTERROGATION
- While teens get snacks or dessert, cast members will circulate. Another option is to hold the pizza until this time.
- When the forms have been turned in, the Detective will go over the incorrect ones first, asking those cast members if they did it. They will deny it. When he gets to Penny, she will admit it and say Ima was going to expose her plan to eliminate pension plans. She put peanut oil in the salad, knowing Ima was allergic to it.

Chapter Five

MIND-BENDING MYSTERY CLUB ACTIVITIES

D
o you have a lot of teen mystery readers in your school or public library? Keeping the momentum going on a teen interest sometimes feels like a mystery itself, but it doesn't have to be! This chapter has ideas and activities for a teen mystery club. Some of these activities have on-line versions if your library doesn't have enough staff members or interested teens to maintain a club that meets regularly. Many activities listed could also work as stand-alone events.

A mystery club can incorporate elements of writing, science, math, collaboration, analysis, and, of course, reading. With enough interest, the members of the Mind-Bending Mystery Club can plan events for other age groups or other teens at the library. Ideas for establishing a club and organizing offshoot events are outlined in this chapter. The chapter also includes some sample scripts and scenes as well as tips for inviting teens to develop their own.

INVESTIGATING THE CRIME SCENE: GAUGING INTEREST IN A TEEN MYSTERY CLUB

Sometimes interest in teen programs is a bit like the chicken-and-egg question. Do teens become interested in a topic because there is a club devoted to it, or is there a club because teens were interested in the topic and started one? Although some teens may develop an interest if they have a club to attend, it is good to find a core group of dedicated teens to help start a new venture.

Run a "favorite genre" poll online and in print to find out if teens are interested in mysteries or thrillers. Ask what favorite series teens read, and also what series they liked when they were younger. The answers will help identify mystery fans.

Set up a display of teen mystery books or establish an online book display and monitor the statistics on those titles. A physical teen mystery book display could include paper footprints leading up to it, "fingerprint" dust and tape, crime scene tape, or even a body outlined on the floor.

Host a special mystery-themed event such as a CSI crime scene night or a mystery dinner and have an evaluation form asking if teens would like to attend more programs like that.

As with any new teen series of programs, the club may take a while to catch on. Give teens at least six months to learn about the new club and begin attending regularly before changing nights, times, or the style of meetings.

SOLVING THE CRIME: MIND-BENDING MYSTERY CLUB ACTIVITIES

MYSTERIOUS SNACKS

Snacks help any meeting get going, and it may be fun to have some Mystery Snacks for teens to taste and report on. For example, offer a fruit they may not be familiar with or a hybrid flavor of juice, popcorn, or chips to identify. Also provide some traditional snacks.

ICE BREAKERS

As teens come in, hand them a message in code to work on as they snack and as latecomers arrive. Begin with a simple alphanumeric code (C = 1, D = 2, etc.) and devise more elaborate ones for future meetings. Give prizes to those teens who figure out the code and the message, or let them design the code and message for the next meeting. More activities for coding are outlined in the following section.

Begin each meeting by mentioning any new teen mystery books or new mystery movies in the library. Invite teens to share any titles they've read and enjoyed—or hated—and why.

If the group is shy at first, conduct a live poll on their favorite childhood detectives. List their choices, such as the Hardy Boys, Scooby-Doo, and so forth, and then talk about why those characters are better than others. For another fun discussion, invite teens to imagine unusual pairings of those characters—for example, Nancy Drew and Scooby-Doo, or a favorite childhood version of the Avengers detectives.

Ask the teens what paranormal power they would like to have to solve crimes. (They cannot choose the ability to instantly know who did something and why.) Or write a variety of superpowers on slips of paper and have each club member draw one. Then everyone has to explain how her or his power would be used for crime solving. If this activity is popular, the group could develop a mystery skit involving all their characters.

CLUB TOPIC: CRUCIAL CODING

Ask teens when they use codes in their lives. (Likely TXTing is their biggest use, but also discuss computers.) Mention how codes are used for national security, and review some of the laws and penalties for hackers to show the relevance. Note that all the Crucial Coding program ideas can transfer online to a social networking page, including the discussion, the links, and the description of how to make invisible inks.

Present information on Navajo code talkers and their work in the past. Discuss the importance of that work and what might have happened without it. Provide books and other materials on the subject. Bring a laptop and let teens look at the Navajo Code Talkers Museum site for more information (www.history.navy .mil/faqs/faq61-4.htm).

Ask teens which books they have read that had characters who used invisible ink. The Harry Potter series is one they may readily mention. Provide white candles and paper and let the teens write messages. Then have them rub crayon over the candle wax to reveal the message. Another method requires lemon juice and a safe warming device. Invite teens to invent invisible inks or messages.

Print the Dancing Men figures from the Sherlock Holmes short story "The Adventure of the Dancing Men" (some online sites have an updated version of this to link to if desired) and have them practice making and solving coded messages. Show the different code fonts available on the computer, too.

In *The Da Vinci Code*, clues are found in some famous paintings. Bring photos of those or others to show, and invite teens to create a drawing with a secret code in it. Nancy Drew often found clues in rugs. Where else could teens hide messages?

CLUB TOPIC: GREAT GADGETS

Identify fictional and real gadgets used in crime solving and provide descriptions of them. (Hint: Use James Bond books or movies as well as the International Spy Museum site at www.spymuseum.org.) Try to obtain some real gadgets—some devices that are common now used to be used for spy hunting, such as the GPS. Ask teens to decide which are real and which are fictional. Invite them to invent a gadget and explain how it would be used in crime fighting. Then they could develop a skit that incorporates their gadgets.

CLUB TOPIC: CRIME SCENES

Set up a mini crime scene at each meeting and invite teens to work out what happened. You can devise a scenario with specific clues, but the object is for teens to creatively figure it out. Give a prize for the most creative explanation. The winners may want to set the scene for the next club meeting.

Sample Scene 1: A teen girl was supposed to meet a friend at the library and has not returned home. Evidence: spilled purse with overturned chair; open cell phone; torn note indicating someone was supposed to meet someone else; chemistry or other textbook left open; drop of blood on paper or hair ribbon to indicate physical violence between two girls, or a shoe left behind.

Sample Scene 2: A boy's stepfather is in the hospital after being poisoned. Evidence: flour dusted on kitchen implements; mysterious bottles; a plant; cookbooks; a book on edible plants; household remedies; a crumpled flier about poison control.

Online Scene: A photo of a girl and guy making out circulates among cell phones at a local high school. Then the boy goes missing. Both were dating other people, but all of them deny knowledge. Another photo of the boy tied up begins to circulate with a deadline of twenty-four hours. What happened and why?

CLUB TOPIC: CRIME SOLVING OF THE FUTURE

Should DNA kits be available at local drugstores? Invite teens to discuss all sides of this issue. Provide data about how long it takes your local county and state to analyze DNA and how much it costs to do so. Provide similar data on other types of evidence.

Explore fund-raising initiatives and other ways that citizens can help with crime fighting.

Discuss why people do not like to come forward during crimes or afterward. Provide information about the case of Kitty Genovese, in which no one responded to her screams as she was stabbed to death.

How many missing persons cases are there in your state? How many are teens? Ask teens for reasons why some people may want to go missing. Discuss the Doe Network (www.doenetwork.org) and how technology is helping with those cases.

CLUB TOPIC: PROFILING AND PATTERNS

Talk about the profiling department of the real FBI and ones on TV. What kinds of classes or topics do profilers study in order to do that work?

Before the meeting, fill a backpack with various items. At the meeting, invite teens to discuss what those items tell about the person.

Log on to Facebook and show teens all the personal, detailed information that can easily be found there.

Describe some serial crimes, either fictional or real, and ask teens to speculate about the criminal.

Bring several descriptions of the first shots fired at Lexington in the American Revolutionary War and discuss how they all conflict. Invite teens to sketch out and describe what happened as a group to show the difficulty of producing an accurate accounting.

CLUB TOPIC: USING ALL SENSES

The children's Halloween party game of putting foods in boxes for players to identify by touch can translate to a teen event. Jello, for example, would be fairly easy to identify. Try different types of cooked and uncooked pasta, cottage cheese, onions, and other foods with more subtle textures.

Flavor sprays that create sweet treats without the calories are popular now. See if teens can identify those flavors sprayed on bread or crackers. Or purchase Jelly Belly candies in a variety of flavors and invite teens to guess what the flavors are.

Bring in three types of flowers as well as three versions of the same flower—freshly cut, a few days old, and a week old. Blindfold volunteers and invite them to smell the flowers and make observations.

Have another staff member run into the room during the meeting, take your purse or wallet, and run out. He or she should say a few gruff things. Give teens two minutes to write down everything they saw and heard, including a detailed description of the "thief."

Answer your cell phone and pretend the call is upsetting or makes you angry. Mention some specific times and dates as well as a few names. At the end of the meeting, invite teens to list what was said as closely as possible.

CLUB TOPIC: GUESTS AND TOURS

Invite local law enforcement personnel to talk about crime or forensics. Speakers could include judges, private detectives, or others connected with solving crimes.

Arrange to have teens tour a local morgue or law enforcement agency or museum. This activity could be expanded with online interviews and photos or short movies of tours.

CLUB ACTIVITY: TRIVIA CONTESTS OR MYSTERIOUS MONDAYS

Mystery lovers enjoy ferreting out clues themselves, and trivia contests will appeal to these teen genre fans. These types of contests are also great to post online or to send through e-mail between meetings or for a virtual version of this club. Five questions are fun without seeming like a homework assignment. Or you could post one question a week, on Mysterious Mondays, to keep teens returning to the social networking site for the mystery club. You could also invite teens to write fictional solutions for crimes.

TRIVIA CONTEST 1: AUTHOR AND BOOK MYSTERIES

1. Agatha Christie once disappeared for a short time. When did she disappear and for how long?
    (Answer: In 1926, Christie went missing for 11 days.)

2. Where does Sherlock Holmes live? Is that street real?
    (Answer: The address is 221B Baker Street, and it is a real street.)

3. The author Lois Duncan wrote about a tragic mystery in her family. What happened and when?
    (Answer: Her 18-year-old daughter, Kaitlyn Arquette, was murdered in 1989.)

4. *A Northern Light* by Jennifer Donnelly is based on a real crime. What happened and when? What other book features this same crime?
    (Answer: The crime was a murder in 1906, which is also featured in Theodore Dreiser's *An American Tragedy*.)

5. What was stolen from Ernest Hemingway in 1922? Was it ever found?
    (Answer: A suitcase full of stories and manuscripts was taken; it was never recovered.)

TRIVIA CONTEST 2: HISTORY MYSTERIES
(THESE DO NOT HAVE DEFINITIVE ANSWERS.)

1. Why do some believe there was a second shooter in the assassination of President Kennedy?

2. What is mysterious about Stonehenge?

3. What is a famous nickname for the Whitechapel murderer? Was the identity of the killer ever discovered?

4. What happened to the Lost Colony of Roanoke?

5. What is the purpose of Area 51? Is it still operating today?

Chapter Six

WHEN BOOK DISCUSSIONS GET MYSTERIOUS

Book discussions can feel like assigned reading without an easy approach and a welcoming setting. It might take a while to attract teens to regularly held book discussions, so you may want to offer online versions or themed discussions to build interest. Once teens are attending, keep them interested by choosing entertaining and compelling books and asking engaging questions. To get things rolling, this chapter provides book discussion questions for all the subgenres of mystery presented in this book. Instead of discussing prearranged questions, however, teens might want to focus on a particular aspect of a book or discuss why an ending does or does not work. Even though they may all want to vent about why they do not like a particular book, their passion for the topic is invaluable. When teens get involved with books, the result is always positive.

Consider offering themed book discussions to encourage shy or reluctant participants. For this type of program, invite teens to bring a book that fits a category. Examples of categories that would fit include "most surprising ending"; any of the subgenres, such as romantic suspense; award winners; classic authors such as Christie, Doyle, or Chandler; and mysteries made into movies.

Group members that have met for a time may want to suggest their own books or themes. This is another sign of success as teens become invested to the point where they lead. Rotating discussion leaders may help this investment continue. Other incentives may include free books for those participating, snacks, and online voting systems for future titles.

INVESTIGATE THESE

Alphin, Elaine Marie. *An Unspeakable Crime: The Prosecution and Persecution of Leo Frank*. Carolrhoda, 2010.
The notable mystery fiction writer accomplishes gripping nonfiction as well with this study of the 1913 murder of Mary Phagan and the subsequent punishment the local community handed down on Leo Frank. Frank's life was tarnished by this crime and his arrest for it. He was finally pardoned in 1986, many decades after his death. Alphin collected anecdotal evidence and original papers to document this compelling book. (Gr. 9+)

1. Do you think her background as a mystery fiction writer helped Alphin write nonfiction about a true crime? In what way?
2. Why wasn't the police department more careful with the blood and hair evidence?
3. Why did the police focus on Leo Frank?
4. Why did the media and public agree with their condemnation?
5. Why did prosecutor Dorsey want to convict Leo Frank rather than Jim Conley?
6. Do you feel Leo Frank's conversations and interactions with Mary Phagan were inappropriate?
7. Do you feel some of the witnesses lied? How and why?
8. Do you feel that cases can grow out of proportion like this today? What could be done to stop it? Why was Frank granted a pardon decades after his death?
9. What do you think Leo Frank meant in his last words when he said, "I think more of my wife and my mother than I do of my own life"?
10. Why were so many high-profile people interested in lynching Leo Frank? Why did so many people come to see his body?

Aronson, Marc. *Master of Deceit: J. Edgar Hoover and America in the Age of Lies*. Candlewick, 2012.
When Martin Luther King Jr. received an anonymous letter, he believed someone was attempting to blackmail him into committing suicide. Aronson makes a credible case that the author of the letter may have been assistant FBI director William Sullivan, who was following J. Edgar Hoover's principles. Fascinating sources provide interesting and thought-provoking reading. Aronson includes a chapter on how he researched this topic. (Gr. 9+)

1. In your opinion, was Dr. King correct in believing that the letter was encouraging him to commit suicide?

2. In chapter 5, Aronson remarks that the political cartoons about the threat of communism were not different in tone from messages about Muslims after the September 11, 2001, attacks. Do you feel he is correct? Were people wrong about communism? About Muslims?
3. Why did the public stop believing Palmer's message of fear?
4. What would have happened if Palmer had run for and been elected president?
5. Why didn't Hoover want the public to know about the innocent people who died in the hunt for John Dillinger? How was he able to keep that out of the news?
6. Do you think things are kept out of the news today? When and how?
7. Why was it dangerous to allow Hoover's work to be private and undisclosed after President Roosevelt extended the FBI's power? Do you think there is legislation today that allows branches of government to be private in the same way?
8. Do you feel the Rosenbergs were innocent? Do you think this country makes arrests based on media-induced fears?
9. Do you feel the FBI could have done something to prevent JFK's death or could have been involved in the death of Malcolm X?
10. What areas of the FBI are important to national security today? What blocks are in place today to prevent the abuse of power?

Griffin, Adele, and Lisa Brown. *Picture the Dead*. Sourcebooks Fire, 2010.
In this richly illustrated story of suspense, Jennie Lovell's twin, Toby, and her fiancé, Will, have been killed in the Civil War. Will's brother, Quinn, returns home a strange man with an unnerving interest in Jennie. She is desperate for a sighting or message from Will as she tries to protect herself from increasing danger. This unusual, multilayered story is perfect for reluctant readers. (Gr. 7+)

1. Do you think Jennie is feeling Toby's presence or Will's presence at the beginning of the story, or no one's?
2. Did your feelings change on that at the end? Why?
3. Why are Jennie's aunt and uncle so unhappy with her?
4. Would Quinn have turned out as he did without the war experience? Do you feel people can change deeply as a result of an experience?
5. Do you think photographers can capture spirits? Why or why not?
6. Why is it so important to Will's family to get a sign from him? How would people suffering great grief over the loss of family members try today to get a sign from them?
7. Do you feel Jennie gets comfort from the presence of Toby or Will? Would such a thing be possible, in your opinion?
8. Which illustrations stood out in your mind after reading the book? Why?

9. What other options do you believe Jennie may have had in that time rather than live with her aunt and uncle?
10. Does she save herself, in your opinion, or does she have help?

Harazin, S. A. *Blood Brothers*. Delacorte, 2007.

This Edgar Award–nominated title follows 17-year-old med tech Clay, who is trying to scrape together money for rent and college while his best friend, Joey, is headed for an Ivy League premed school, courtesy of his parents. After a shift in the ER, Clay finds Joey disoriented and violent. Joey collapses into a coma at the hospital, and the police, wondering who gave Joey drugs, become interested in Clay. Clay is a loyal friend and uses all his knowledge to uncover what is happening to Joey. He also questions other teens to learn what really happened to his friend. Both the medical setting and Clay himself are dynamic and unique, and this title will appeal to older teens. (Gr. 9+)

1. Would Joey have killed Clay if Clay had not pushed him off in the trailer?
2. Is Clay's father doing a good job as a parent? Why or why not?
3. Does Clay's sister, Darcy, give him good advice about the situation with Joey? Why or why not?
4. Why is Clay fired from the hospital job?
5. Do you think Clay will succeed in becoming a doctor?
6. Is Joey a good friend to Clay before he takes the drugs?
7. Why don't the teens include Clay in the party?
8. Why does Clay like Michelle?
9. Could you do the tasks Clay does for his job? What do you feel is his hardest task?
10. Did you figure out who got the drugs and what they could possibly have been laced with? How? Which scenes in the book helped you figure it out?

Henderson, Lauren. *Kiss Me Kill Me* (Scarlett Wakefield series). Delacorte, 2008.

After a boy dies during their first kiss, Scarlett transfers to the school her family runs, Wakefield Hall, ready to put the tragedy behind her. But someone knows that there is more to the incident than an allergic reaction gone horribly wrong. An anonymous note inspires Scarlett to find out what really happened in this British mystery. (Gr. 8–12)

1. Is it a good idea to kiss someone you just met? Why or why not?
2. Is this a plausible way to kill someone? It is partially based on a real event, but does Henderson make this situation believable?
3. Were you satisfied with the ending, or do you think the author was setting you up for a series?

4. How does the culture in which Scarlett lives and goes to school differ from that in the United States?
5. Would you want to go to Wakefield Hall? Why or why not?
6. Does Scarlett worry about impressing the wrong types? Why do you think so?
7. Why, do you think, would someone want to kill this boy?
8. Do you think his death was really Scarlett's fault?
9. Who do you think wrote the note?
10. What would you do to prove your innocence if this case proved to be murder?

Juby, Susan. *Getting the Girl: A Guide to Private Investigation, Surveillance and Cookery.* **HarperTeen, 2008.**
Freshman Sherman Mack wants to keep a low profile at his high school. He wants to do well in cooking class and admire crush Dini from afar. He wants nothing to do with the Defiling system at his school—if a girl's photo appears with a *D* in the bathrooms, the rest of the students act as if she is invisible. Lots of girls have transferred after being Defiled. Sherman realizes it is often the quieter girls who date popular boys who get Defiled. He worries about Dini after she starts seeing popular athlete Lester. When his mystery-loving friend, Vanessa, wants him to find out who is behind Defiling, Sherman reluctantly begins to track down clues. When Vanessa gets Defiled, he realizes he needs to take serious steps to stop the entire practice. (Gr. 6–9)

1. What would you do if you were Defiled?
2. What would be upsetting enough to cause someone to change schools?
3. Why does Vanessa want to know who is behind the Defiling?
4. What do you think someone who is Defiled should do? Is there an adult you could trust at your school to help stop bullying?
5. Did you know who was behind the Defiling? How did you figure it out? If not, who did you think was behind it?
6. Did you enjoy Sherman's plan to unveil the person behind the bullying?
7. Do Sherman's plans work the way he expects? Why or why not?
8. Why is Sherman a hero? What character traits make him one?
9. Why does he like Dini? Why doesn't Dini get Defiled?
10. Does any form of online bullying seem like Defiling?

Peacock, Kathleen. *Hemlock*. **HarperCollins, 2012.**
In this first book of a planned trilogy, MacKenzie is still trying to manage months after her best friend, Amy, was murdered by a werewolf in their small town of Hemlock. Amy's boyfriend Jason's behavior has turned dark, and Kyle, the fourth in their group, is also being mysterious. A tracker group moves into town to kill the werewolves, but Mac's dreams about Amy tell her that is the wrong answer. Mac is attacked by a tracker, who threatens her to not talk about it. She is also saved by a werewolf that turns out to be someone she knows. Mac's desire to find out what happened to her friend while sorting through her romantic feelings for Kyle and her confused feelings for Jason make this story a realistic, engrossing teen tale. (Gr. 7+)

1. Why does Mac still dream that Amy is telling her something?
2. Should Jason feel guilty about breaking up with Amy the night she was killed?
3. Is Kyle dangerous to Mac?
4. Why is the trackers' work wrong?
5. What would be a good solution for the werewolves?
6. When in history have people tried to force other people into camps such as the ones in this story for the werewolves?
7. Are camps a solution? Why or why not?
8. Does this volume provide answers?
9. Who are the villains in this story? When did you realize they were?
10. Is Jason good or bad? Why?

Poznanski, Ursula. *Erebos*. **Annick Press, 2010.**
Nick is given a disc for an online role-playing game that pulls him in with riveting fights and challenges. Then the computer seems to know what he is doing when he is not playing, and soon it is sending him on missions in real life. He does not know whom to trust as he tries to find out about the game and its dark secrets in this international award–winning title. (Gr. 9+)

1. Do you like role-playing games? Why or why not?
2. Why does Nick like the game?
3. Why does he agree to recruit more players?
4. Do you agree with the friends who did not want to play?
5. What is a good amount of time to play a new game? When does it start to get obsessive?

6. Do you think computers could get smarter and learn about your life, as Erebos does?
7. Are there any technologies you use now that learn about you or remember your preferences?
8. How did you feel about the ending with Aidan's father's message?
9. What made this game dangerous?
10. Are there other games that are not online that could get out of control like this?

Renn, Diana. *Tokyo Heist.* **Viking, 2012.**
Manga-loving Violet thinks her dreams have come true when she has to go with her father to Japan. But soon she is involved in solving an international art crime as she tracks down clues so her father will not be in danger. Details of Japanese culture and life richly enhance the modern setting. Violet works on her own manga story while taking part in an exciting caper in this well-crafted tale. (Gr. 7–10)

Program note: Before the discussion begins, offer Pocky or other Japanese-themed snacks.

1. Why does Violet distrust Skye at first?
2. At the end, Reika says Violet helped her as well. Is there anything in the story that gives readers a clue that Reika is not happy in Japan?
3. Could this story have taken place in Seattle? How do the details of Japanese life and culture enhance the story?
4. Did you believe Yoshi was the leak? Why or why not?
5. Did you know who the villain was in this story? Why is Reika attracted to him?
6. What could Violet have done to improve her relationship with her father?
7. How does Reika help Violet improve her story? Is it important to get opinions from other people on creative work? Why or why not?
8. What does Violet do that surprised you in order to solve the crime? Could you have done something similar? What if your family members were in danger?
9. Violet often says that lives are more important than art. When is art really important? How does it help people?
10. Did you find the ending with Edge believable? Would you have been happy if that relationship was not resolved in a positive manner?

Silvey, Craig. *Jasper Jones.* **Knopf, 2009.**
Thirteen-year-old Charlie is summoned into the night by school dropout Jasper
Jones, who needs Charlie's help covering up a murder. Jasper found the body of his
girlfriend, Laura, hanging from a tree and knows he will be blamed. He and Charlie
bury her until they can figure out who did this. In the process, Charlie uncovers
ugliness in his mining town, from prejudice against his best friend, Vietnamese
Jeffrey, to secrets among the town pillars and even to fissures in his own house. Set
in 1965 Australia, this Printz Honor Award title is filled with excellent writing and
surprises. (Gr. 9+)

1. When did you get a sense that this story is set in the past?
2. What makes it clear that this story takes place in another country?
3. Why does Jasper Jones choose Charlie to help him with Laura's body?
4. Why are Jeffrey and Charlie such good friends?
5. Could you keep hiding a body in secret in this case, with a good reason?
6. Why does the town believe Mad Jack is crazy?
7. Do you think Charlie will leave town in the future and not return?
8. Will his father become a published author? Will Charlie?
9. What will become of Jeffrey's family?
10. Will people in the town realize that the Sarge and Laura/Eliza's father are
    bad? What do you think will happen to them?
11. Why do you think this book received the Printz Honor Award?

Chapter Seven

IT'S NO MYSTERY TO MARKET

Mystery readers especially like to uncover clues and find out things for themselves. So marketing great titles to them can be effective even in stealth . . . Effective marketing makes finding out about mystery books and programs just as much fun as the books or events themselves. Try some of these techniques to bring readers to the books or to events focused on their favorite genre.

BURIED BOOKMARKS

There are many ways to use "buried" bookmarks in the teen collection. One way is to hide a bookmark instructing the finder to bring it to the nearest service point for a prize. You will have to promote the existence of the bookmark, which can lead to even more mess than usual in a busy collection, and a notice will have to be put up each time the bookmark is found, but the activity can be a fun promotion for Teen Read Week or National Library Week. It may be a good idea to hide a couple each day in case someone other than a teen picks it up and tosses it.

Another way to use hidden bookmarks is to put a web address or QR code on the bookmark that will send the reader to a special site where further instructions await. The reward could be a treasure map, a list of great mysteries to read, an advertisement for an upcoming event, or a coupon for money off fines that the teen could print and use.

Bookmarks can also be printed with coupons for extra checkouts of media beyond the limit or money off fines. There is no guarantee that winners will let staff know until they use the coupon bookmarks, but several could be hidden at once. Coupons could be limited to one per teen to avoid having one young person finding all the prizes.

Yet another buried bookmark variation is to write instructions in code or invisible ink indicating where teens can obtain small prizes. To write an invisible message, simply use a small, white candle. Teens can rub crayons over the wax to see the message. Or use a simple alphanumeric code and post the key or a hint each day on the teen website.

PERPLEXING PUZZLES

HIDDEN PUZZLE PIECES

Print out program information, a book list, or a coupon for money off fines on a piece of paper and cut copies of it into puzzle pieces. Ellison or other die-cutter companies offer puzzle shapes. Put the pieces in several bowls or envelopes and place them at various service points. Teens who ask for a puzzle piece or who answer a library trivia question will receive a piece.

Another option is to place all the pieces at one service point. Teens who return a book-review form each week during the summer or school year will receive a puzzle piece and a small prize.

PUZZLING PROGRAMS

To keep momentum going for a series of programs with a mystery theme, offer teens a puzzle piece after each event. Those who attend several events will have a completed puzzle, which can be a prize coupon or a form that can be turned in for a prize.

Another option is to promote the final mystery program event (or a summer or end-of-the-school-year event) by putting only one piece of information, such as the date or time, on each puzzle piece. Teens who complete the puzzle will win a special door prize at the final event.

FEVERISH FOOTPRINTS

Use a die-cutting machine to cut several footprints. With nonpermanent fixative, apply the footprints to the floor or wall to attract and direct teens to a program or to a display of books and media on mysteries. Use crime scene tape to decorate the program room or to outline the display.

MYSTERIOUS MARKS

Feature mystery books in the collection by attaching stick-on gems or fingerprints or magnifying-glass stickers to make them stand out. Or put QR codes on mystery books to send teens to a site listing more great mystery reads or to an online mystery discussion group.

TITLES AND SERIES BY SUBGENRE

REALISTIC MYSTERIES

▶ UNDAUNTED DETECTIVES

Carter, Ally. *Heist Society* (Heist Society series). Hyperion, 2010.

Cortez. Sarah. *You Don't Have a Clue: Latino Mystery Stories for Teens*. Piñata Books for Young Readers, 2011.

Fredericks, Mariah. *Crunch Time*. Atheneum Books for Young Readers, 2007.

Grisham, John. *Theodore Boone: Kid Lawyer* (Theodore Boone series). Puffin, 2011.

McClintock, Norah. *Dooley Takes the Fall* (Ryan Dooley Mysteries). Red Deer Press, 2008.

McGowan, Anthony. *The Knife That Killed Me*. Delacorte, 2010.

Neri, G., and Randy DuBurke. *Yummy: The Last Days of a Southside Shorty*. Lee and Low, 2010.

Reid, Kimberly. *My Own Worst Frenemy* (Langdon Prep series). Dafina, 2011.

Renn, Diana. *Tokyo Heist*. Viking, 2012.

Shoemaker, Tim. *Code of Silence* (Code of Silence series). Zondervan, 2012.

Stratton, Allan. *Borderline*. HarperCollins, 2010.

▶ ADULT REALISTIC MYSTERY BOOKS FOR TEENS

Barr, Nevada. *Track of the Cat* (Anna Pigeon series). Putnam, 1993.

Ferraris, Zoe. *Finding Nouf* (A Katya Hijazi and Nayir al-Sharqi Novel). Houghton Mifflin, 2008.

Lupton, Rosamund. *Sister: A Novel*. Broadway, 2011.

▶ ACCUSED TEENS

Fusili, Jim. *Marley Z and the Bloodstained Violin*. Dutton, 2008.

Godwin, Jane. *Falling from Grace*. Holiday House, 2007.

Henderson, Lauren. *Kiss Me Kill Me* (Scarlett Wakefield series). Delacorte, 2008.

Jones, Patrick. *Cheated*. Walker, 2008.

Ludwig, Elisa. *Pretty Crooked* (Pretty Crooked Trilogy). HarperCollins, 2012.

Runholt, Susan. *The Mystery of the Third Lucretia* (Kari + Lucas Mystery series). Puffin, 2009.

Schrefer, Eliot. *The Deadly Sister*. Scholastic, 2010.

▶ DISAPPEARING FAMILY AND FRIENDS

Abrahams, Peter. *Reality Check*. HarperTeen, 2010.

Bradbury, Jennifer. *Shift*. Atheneum, 2008.

Brooks, Kevin. *Black Rabbit Summer*. Chicken House (Scholastic), 2008.

Burak, Kathryn. *Emily's Dress and Other Missing Things*. Roaring Brook Press, 2012.

Cooney, Caroline B. *If the Witness Lied*. Delacorte, 2009.

Gerber, Linda. *The Death by Bikini Mysteries* (The Death by . . . Mysteries series). Speak (Penguin), 2011.

Green, John. *Paper Towns*. Dutton, 2008.

Henry, April. *Girl, Stolen*. Henry Holt, 2010.

Henry, April. *The Night She Disappeared*. Henry Holt, 2012.

Northrup, Michael. *Gentlemen*. Scholastic, 2009.

Plum-Ucci, Carol. *Following Christopher Creed*. Harcourt, 2011.

Shepard, Sara. *The Lying Game* (Lying Game series). HarperTeen, 2011.

Shepard, Sara. *Pretty Little Liars* (Pretty Little Liars series). HarperTeen, 2006.

Taylor, Brooke. *Undone*. Walker, 2008.

Valentine, Jenny. *Me, the Missing and the Dead*. HarperTeen, 2008.

Weingarten, Lynn. *Wherever Nina Lies*. Point (Scholastic), 2009.

▶ SMALL-TOWN SLEUTHS

Abrahams, Peter. *Down the Rabbit Hole* (Echo Falls Mystery series). HarperCollins, 2006.

Beaufrand, Mary Jane. *The River*. Little, Brown, 2010.

Ford, John C. *The Morgue and Me*. Viking, 2009.

Hautman, Pete, and Mary Logue. *Snatched* (Bloodwater series). Putnam Juvenile, 2006.

Mackall, Dandi Daley. *The Silence of Murder*. Knopf, 2011.

Parker, Robert. *The Boxer and the Spy*. Philomel, 2008.

Pfeffer, Susan Beth. *Blood Wounds*. Harcourt Children's Books, 2011.

Reiss, Kathryn. *Blackthorn Winter*. Harcourt, 2006.

Rosenfield, Kat. *Amelia Anne Is Dead and Gone*. Dutton, 2012.

Strasser, Todd. *Kill You Last* (The Thrillogy series). Egmont, 2011.

▶ HUMOROUS INSPECTORS, OR WHAT'S SO FUNNY ABOUT CRIME?

Beaudoin, Sean. *You Killed Wesley Payne*. Little, Brown, 2011.

Berk, Josh. *The Dark Days of Hamburger Halpin*. Knopf, 2010.

Ferraiolo, Jack D. *The Big Splash* (Big Splash series). Amulet Books, 2011.

Jinks, Catherine. *The Reformed Vampire Support Group*. Harcourt, 2009.

Juby, Susan. *Getting the Girl: A Guide to Private Investigation, Surveillance and Cookery*. HarperTeen, 2008.

King, A. S. *Please Ignore Vera Dietz*. Knopf, 2010.

Leck, James. *The Adventures of Jack Lime*. Kids Can Press, 2010.

Low, Dene. *Petronella Saves Nearly Everyone: The Entomological Tales of Augustus T. Percival.* Houghton Mifflin, 2009.

Moriarty, Jaclyn. *The Murder of Bindy MacKenzie.* Arthur A. Levine Books, 2006.

Pauley, Kimberly. *Cat Girl's Day Off.* Tu Books (Lee and Low), 2012.

▶ SPORTY SLEUTHS

Abrahams, Peter. *Bullet Point.* HarperTeen, 2010.

Abrahams, Peter. *Down the Rabbit Hole.* (Echo Falls Mystery series). HarperCollins, 2006.

Bloor, Edward. *Tangerine: Tenth-Anniversary Edition.* Harcourt, 2007.

Bradbury, Jennifer. *Shift.* Atheneum, 2008.

Feinstein, John. *Last Shot* (Final Four Mystery series). Knopf, 2005.

Parker, Robert. *The Boxer and the Spy.* Philomel, 2008.

HIGH-TECH WHODUNITS

▶ CSI TEENS

Chibbaro, Julie. *Deadly.* Atheneum Books for Young Readers, 2011.

Ferguson, Alane. *The Christopher Killer* (Forensic Mysteries series). Perfection Learning, 2008.

Ford, John C. *The Morgue and Me.* Viking, 2009.

Harazin, S. A. *Blood Brothers.* Delacorte, 2007.

Reichs, Kathy. *Virals* (Virals series). Razorbill, 2010.

Yancey, Rick. *The Monstrumologist* (The Monstrumologist series). Simon and Schuster Books for Young Readers, 2010.

▶ FUTURISTIC MYSTERIES

Bloor, Edward. *Tangerine: Tenth-Anniversary Edition.* Harcourt, 2007.

Haddix, Margaret Peterson. *FOUND* (The Missing series). Simon and Schuster, 2009.

Henderson, J. A. *Bunker 10.* Harcourt, 2007.

Pearson, Mary. *The Adoration of Jenna Fox* (The Jenna Fox Chronicles series). Henry Holt, 2008.

Roth, Veronica. *Divergent* (Divergent series). Katharine Tegen Books, 2012.

Shusterman, Neal. *Unwind* (Unwind Dystology series). Simon and Schuster Books for Young Readers, 2007.

▶ INTERNET, COMPUTER, AND SPY CAPERS

Carter, Ally. *I'd Tell You I Love You, but Then I'd Have to Kill You* (Gallagher Girls series). Hyperion, 2007.

Child, Lauren. *Ruby Redfort: Look Into My Eyes.* Candlewick, 2011.

Greenland, Shannon. *Model Spy* (The Specialists series). Puffin, 2007.

Horowitz, Anthony. *Stormbreaker* (Alex Rider series). Philomel, 2001.

Jinks, Catherine. *Evil Genius* (The Evil Genius series). Harcourt, 2007.

Patterson, James. *The Angel Experiment* (Maximum Ride series). Little, Brown, 2005.

Poznanski, Ursula. *Erebos*. Annick Press, 2010.

❯ ADULT AUTHOR FOR TEENS
Reich, Christopher.

THRILLERS

❯ THRILLING READING
Abrahams, Peter. *Bullet Point*. HarperTeen, 2010.

Abrahams, Peter. *Reality Check*. HarperTeen, 2010.

Cadnum, Michael. *Seize the Storm*. Farrar, Straus and Giroux, 2012.

Cooney, Caroline B. *Diamonds in the Shadow*. Waterbrook Press, 2007.

Evans, Richard Paul. *Michael Vey: The Prisoner of Cell 25* (Michael Vey series). Mercury Ink/Simon Pulse, 2011.

Giles, Gail. *What Happened to Cass McBride?* Little, Brown, 2007.

Price, Charlie. *Desert Angel*. Farrar, Straus and Giroux, 2011.

Roth, Veronica. *Divergent* (Divergent series). Katharine Tegen Books, 2012.

Sedgwick, Marcus. *White Crow*. Roaring Brook Press, 2011.

Shusterman, Neal. *Unwind* (Unwind Dystology series). Simon and Schuster Books for Young Readers, 2007.

Smith, Alexander Gordon. *Lockdown* (Escape from Furnace series). Farrar, Straus and Giroux, 2009.

Wynne-Jones, Tim. *Blink and Caution*. Candlewick, 2011.

FANTASTIC AND PARANORMAL MYSTERIES

❯ SUPERSLEUTHS AND SPECIAL POWERS
Bray, Libba. *The Diviners*. Little, Brown, 2012.

Cusick, Richie Tankersley. *Spirit Walk: Walk of the Spirits and Shadow Mirror*. Speak, 2013.

Derting, Kimberly. *The Body Finder* (The Body Finder Novels series). Harper, 2010.

Gier, Kerstin. *Ruby Red* (Ruby Red series). Henry Holt, 2011.

Harrington, Kim. *Clarity* (Clarity Novels series). Point, 2011.

Hodkin, Michelle. *The Unbecoming of Mara Dyer* (The Mara Dyer Trilogy). Simon and Schuster, 2011.

Johnson, Maureen. *The Name of the Star* (The Shades of London series). Putnam, 2011.

Layman, John, and Rob Guillory. *Chew: Volume 1, Taster's Choice* (Chew series). Image Comics, 2009.

McMann, Lisa. *Wake* (Wake Trilogy). Simon Pulse, 2008.

Olsen, Greg. *Envy* (Empty Coffin series). Splinter, 2011.

Pauley, Kimberly. *Cat Girl's Day Off.* Tu Books (Lee and Low), 2012.

Perez, Marlene. *Dead Is the New Black* (Dead Is series). Graphia, 2008.

Staub, Wendy Corsi. *Lily Dale Awakening* (Lily Dale series). Walker, 2007.

Ward, Rachel. *Numbers* (Numbers series). Chicken House, 2010.

❱ ADULT SUPERSLEUTHS AND SPECIAL POWERS BOOKS FOR TEENS

Fforde, Jasper. *The Eyre Affair* (Thursday Next Novels). Viking, 2002.

Hamilton, Steve. *The Lock Artist.* Minotaur Books, 2010.

Laurie, Victoria. *Abby Cooper, Psychic Eye* (Psychic Eye Mysteries series). Signet, 2004.

❱ DARK FORCES

Dashner, James. *The Maze Runner* (Maze Runner series). Delacorte, 2009.

Ford, Michael. *The Poisoned House.* Albert Whitman, 2011.

Healey, Karen. *The Shattering.* Little, Brown, 2011.

McMann, Lisa. *Cryer's Cross.* Simon Pulse, 2011.

Miller, Barnabas, and Jordan Orlando. *7 Souls.* Random House Children's Books, 2010.

Mitchell, Saundra. *Shadowed Summer.* Delacorte, 2009.

Suma, Nova Ren. *Imaginary Girls.* Dutton, 2011.

Wooding, Chris. *Malice* (Malice series). Scholastic, 2010.

❱ VOICES FROM THE BEYOND

Armstrong, Kelly. *The Summoning* (Darkest Powers series). HarperCollins, 2008.

Grabenstein, Chris. *The Crossroads* (Haunted Mystery series). Yearling Books, 2008.

Griffin, Adele, and Lisa Brown. *Picture the Dead.* Sourcebooks Fire, 2010.

King, A. S. *Please Ignore Vera Dietz.* Knopf, 2010.

Maguire, Eden. *Beautiful Dead: Jonas* (Beautiful Dead series). Sourcebooks Fire, 2010.

Price, Charlie. *Dead Connection.* Roaring Brook Press, 2006.

Riggs, Ransom. *Miss Peregrine's Home for Peculiar Children.* Quirk Books, 2011.

Stolarz, Laurie Faria. *Project 17.* Hyperion, 2007.

Warman, Jessica. *Between.* Walker, 2011.

❱ CREATURES WITH CLUES

Beaudoin, Sean. *Infects.* Candlewick, 2012.

Bowler, Tim. *Buried Thunder.* Holiday House, 2011.

Jinks, Catherine. *The Reformed Vampire Support Group.* Harcourt, 2009.

Peacock, Kathleen. *Hemlock* (Hemlock series). HarperCollins, 2012.

Taylor, Laini. *Daughter of Smoke and Bone* (Daughter of Smoke and Bone series). Little, Brown, 2011.

Weston, Robert Paul. *Dust City*. Razorbill, 2010.

MYSTERIES IN TIME AND PLACE

▶ HISTORICAL MYSTERIES

Arnold, Tedd. *Rat Life*. Sleuth (Penguin Group), 2007.

Baratz-Logstead, Lauren. *The Twin's Daughter*. Bloomsbury, 2010.

Blundell, Judy. *Strings Attached*. Scholastic, 2011.

Blundell, Judy. *What I Saw and How I Lied*. Scholastic, 2008.

Bradbury, Jennifer. *Wrapped*. Atheneum, 2011.

Bray, Libba. *The Diviners*. Little, Brown, 2012.

Campbell, Eddie. *The Black Diamond Detective Agency*. First Second, 2007.

Chibbaro, Julie. *Deadly*. Atheneum Books for Young Readers, 2011.

Doyle, Marissa. *Bewitching Season* (Leland Sisters series). Square Fish, 2009.

Dunlap, Susanne. *The Musician's Daughter*. Bloomsbury, 2008.

Elliott, Patricia. *The Pale Assassin*. Holiday House, 2009.

Ford, Michael. *The Poisoned House*. Albert Whitman, 2011.

Griffin, Adele, and Lisa Brown. *Picture the Dead*. Sourcebooks Fire, 2010.

Haines, Kathryn Miller. *The Girl Is Murder*. (The Iris Anderson series). Roaring Brook Press, 2011.

Hoffman, Mary. *The Falconer's Knot: A Story of Friars, Flirtation and Foul Play*. Bloomsbury, 2007.

Lee, Y. S. *The Agency: A Spy in the House* (A Mary Quinn Mystery). Candlewick, 2009.

Low, Dene. *Petronella Saves Nearly Everyone: The Entomological Tales of Augustus T. Percival*. Houghton Mifflin, 2009.

MacLean, Sarah. *The Season*. Orchard Books, 2009.

Riggs, Ransom. *Miss Peregrine's Home for Peculiar Children*. Quirk Books, 2011.

Sedgwick, Marcus. *Revolver*. Roaring Brook Press, 2010.

Silvey, Craig. *Jasper Jones*. Knopf, 2009.

Welsh, T. K. *Resurrection Men*. Dutton, 2007.

Yancey, Rick. *The Monstrumologist* (The Monstrumologist series). Simon and Schuster Books for Young Readers, 2010.

▶ ADULT HISTORICAL MYSTERY SERIES FOR TEENS

Hyzy, Julie. *State of the Onion* (White House Chef Mysteries series). Berkley, 2008.

McCleary, Carol. *The Alchemy of Murder* (Murder series). Forge, 2010.

Winspear, Jacqueline. *Maisie Dobbs* (Maisie Dobbs Mysteries). Penguin, 2004.

▶ JAMES BOND AND SHERLOCK HOLMES REVISITED

Higson, Charlie. *SilverFin: A James Bond Adventure* (Young Bond series). Ian Fleming Publications/Hyperion, 2005.

Lane, Andrew. *Death Cloud*. (Sherlock Holmes: The Legend Begins series). Farrar, Straus and Giroux, 2010.

Scheier, Leah. *Secret Letters*. Hyperion, 2012.

Springer, Nancy. *The Case of the Missing Marquess* (Enola Holmes Mysteries). Philomel, 2006.

▶ ADULT SHERLOCK HOLMES REVISITED SERIES FOR TEENS

Horowitz, Anthony. *House of Silk: A Sherlock Holmes Novel* (Sherlock Holmes series). Mulholland Books, 2011.

▶ YOUNG SLEUTHS FROM POPULAR CONTEMPORARY ADULT SERIES

Coben, Harlan. *Shelter* (A Mickey Bolitar Novel). Putnam, 2011.

Parker, Robert B. *Chasing the Bear: A Young Spenser Novel*. Philomel, 2009.

Wilson, F. Paul. *Jack: Secret Histories* (Young Repairman Jack series). Tor Teen, 2009.

▶ MYSTERIOUS FLASHBACKS AND TIME TRAVEL

Archer, Jennifer. *Through Her Eyes*. HarperTeen, 2011.

Asher, Jay. *Thirteen Reasons Why*. Razorbill, 2007.

Bick, Ilsa. *Draw the Dark*. Carolrhoda, 2010.

Gier, Kerstin. *Ruby Red* (Ruby Red series). Henry Holt, 2011.

Hahn, Mary Downing. *Mister Death's Blue-Eyed Girls*. Clarion, 2012.

Henderson, J. A. *Bunker 10*. Harcourt, 2007.

Johnston, Jeffry. *Fragments*. Simon Pulse, 2007.

Larbalestier, Justine. *Liar*. Bloomsbury, 2009.

Lynch, Chris. *Kill Switch*. Simon and Schuster, 2012.

MacCready, Robin Merrow. *Buried*. Dutton Juvenile, 2006.

Meldrum, Christina. *Madapple*. Knopf, 2008.

Miller, Barnabas, and Jordan Orlando. *7 Souls*. Random House Children's Books, 2010.

Nixon, Joan Lowery. *The Other Side of Dark*. Delacorte (reprint), 2011.

Price, Charlie. *The Interrogation of Gabriel James*. Farrar, Straus and Giroux, 2010.

Reiss, Kathryn. *Blackthorn Winter*. Harcourt, 2006.

Summer, Courtney. *Fall for Anything*. St. Martin's Griffin, 2010.

Tullson, Diane. *Riley Park*. Orca Soundings, 2009.

Warman, Jessica. *Between*. Walker, 2011.

▶ COLD CASES AND LOCKED DOORS

Citra, Becky. *Missing*. Orca, 2011.

Dowd, Siobhan. *The London Eye Mystery*. David Fickling Books, 2008.

McMann, Lisa. *Dead to You.* Simon Pulse, 2012.
Plum-Ucci, Carol. *The Night My Sister Went Missing.* Harcourt, 2008.

ROMANTIC SUSPENSE

Baratz-Logstead, Lauren. *The Twin's Daughter.* Bloomsbury, 2010.
Blundell, Judy. *What I Saw and How I Lied.* Scholastic, 2008.
Cusick, Richie Tankersley. *Spirit Walk: Walk of the Spirits and Shadow Mirror.* Speak, 2013.
Derting, Kimberly. *The Body Finder* (The Body Finder Novels series). Harper, 2010.
Downham, Jenny. *You Against Me.* David Fickling Books, 2011.
Gerber, Linda. *The Death by Bikini Mysteries* (The Death by . . . Mysteries series). Speak (Penguin), 2011.
Henry, April. *The Night She Disappeared.* Henry Holt, 2012.
Hoffman, Mary. *The Falconer's Knot: A Story of Friars, Flirtation and Foul Play.* Bloomsbury, 2007.
Ludwig, Elisa. *Pretty Crooked* (Pretty Crooked Trilogy). HarperCollins, 2012.
MacLean, Sarah. *The Season.* Orchard Books, 2009.
Peacock, Kathleen. *Hemlock* (Hemlock series). HarperCollins, 2012.

▶ **ADULT ROMANTIC SUSPENSE BOOKS FOR TEENS**

Cabot, Meg. *Size 12 Is Not Fat* (Heather Wells series). William Morrow Paperbacks, 2005.
Mason, Sarah. *Playing James.* Ballantine Books, 2004.

NONFICTION AND TRUE CRIME

Alphin, Elaine Marie. *An Unspeakable Crime: The Prosecution and Persecution of Leo Frank.* Carolrhoda, 2010.
Aronson, Marc. *Master of Deceit: J. Edgar Hoover and America in the Age of Lies.* Candlewick, 2012.
Bartoletti, Susan. *They Called Themselves the K.K.K.* Houghton Mifflin, 2010.
Barton, Chris. *Can I See Your ID? True Stories of False Identities.* Dial, 2011.
Blumenthal, Karen. *Bootleg: Murder, Moonshine, and the Lawless Years of Prohibition.* Flash Point/Roaring Brook Press, 2011.
Bowers, Rick. *Spies of Mississippi: The True Story of the Spy Network That Tried to Destroy the Civil Rights Movement.* National Geographic Society, 2010.
Cullen, Dave. *Columbine.* Twelve, 2009.
Janeczko, Paul. *The Dark Game: True Spy Stories.* Candlewick, 2010.
Sheinkin, Steve. *The Notorious Benedict Arnold: A True Story of Adventure, Heroism, and Treachery.* Flash Point/Roaring Brook Press, 2011.

TITLES AND SERIES BY AUTHOR

Abrahams, Peter. *Bullet Point*. HarperTeen, 2010.

———. *Down the Rabbit Hole* (Echo Falls Mystery series). HarperCollins, 2006.

———. *Reality Check*. HarperTeen, 2010.

Alphin, Elaine Marie. *An Unspeakable Crime: The Prosecution and Persecution of Leo Frank*. Carolrhoda, 2010.

Archer, Jennifer. *Through Her Eyes*. HarperTeen, 2011.

Armstrong, Kelly. *The Summoning* (Darkest Powers series). HarperCollins, 2008.

Arnold, Tedd. *Rat Life*. Sleuth (Penguin Group), 2007.

Aronson, Marc. *Master of Deceit: J. Edgar Hoover and America in the Age of Lies*. Candlewick, 2012.

Asher, Jay. *Thirteen Reasons Why*. Razorbill, 2007.

Baratz-Logstead, Lauren. *The Twin's Daughter*. Bloomsbury, 2010.

Barr, Nevada. *Track of the Cat* (Anna Pigeon series). Putnam, 1993. (Adult Series for Teens)

Bartoletti, Susan. *They Called Themselves the K.K.K.* Houghton Mifflin, 2010.

Barton, Chris. *Can I See Your ID? True Stories of False Identities*. Dial, 2011.

Beaudoin, Sean. *Infects*. Candlewick, 2012.

———. *You Killed Wesley Payne*. Little, Brown, 2011.

Beaufrand, Mary Jane. *The River*. Little, Brown, 2010.

Berk, Josh. *The Dark Days of Hamburger Halpin*. Knopf, 2010.

Bick, Ilsa. *Draw the Dark*. Carolrhoda, 2010.

Bloor, Edward. *Tangerine: Tenth-Anniversary Edition*. Harcourt, 2007.

Blumenthal, Karen. *Bootleg: Murder, Moonshine, and the Lawless Years of Prohibition*. Flash Point/Roaring Brook Press, 2011.

Blundell, Judy. *Strings Attached*. Scholastic, 2011.

———. *What I Saw and How I Lied*. Scholastic, 2008.

Bowers, Rick. *Spies of Mississippi: The True Story of the Spy Network That Tried to Destroy the Civil Rights Movement*. National Geographic Society, 2010.

Bowler, Tim. *Buried Thunder*. Holiday House, 2011.

Bradbury, Jennifer. *Shift*. Atheneum, 2008.

———. *Wrapped*. Atheneum, 2011.

Bray, Libba. *The Diviners*. Little, Brown, 2012.

Brooks, Kevin. *Black Rabbit Summer*. Chicken House (Scholastic), 2008.

Burak, Kathryn. *Emily's Dress and Other Missing Things.* Roaring Brook Press, 2012.

Cabot, Meg. *Size 12 Is Not Fat* (Heather Wells series). William Morrow Paperbacks, 2005. (Adult Series for Teens)

Cadnum, Michael. *Seize the Storm.* Farrar, Straus and Giroux, 2012.

Campbell, Eddie. *The Black Diamond Detective Agency.* First Second, 2007.

Carter, Ally. *Heist Society* (Heist Society series). Hyperion, 2010.

———. *I'd Tell You I Love You, but Then I'd Have to Kill You* (Gallagher Girls series). Hyperion, 2007.

Chibbaro, Julie. *Deadly.* Atheneum Books for Young Readers, 2011.

Child, Lauren. *Ruby Redfort: Look Into My Eyes.* Candlewick, 2011.

Citra, Becky. *Missing.* Orca, 2011.

Coben, Harlan. *Shelter* (A Mickey Bolitar Novel). Putnam, 2011.

Cooney, Caroline B. *Diamonds in the Shadow.* Waterbrook Press, 2007.

———. *If the Witness Lied.* Delacorte, 2009.

Cortez, Sarah. *You Don't Have a Clue: Latino Mystery Stories for Teens.* Piñata Books for Young Readers, 2011.

Cullen, Dave. *Columbine.* Twelve, 2009.

Cusick, Richie Tankersley. *Spirit Walk: Walk of the Spirits and Shadow Mirror.* Speak, 2013.

Dashner, James. *The Maze Runner* (Maze Runner series). Delacorte, 2009.

Derting, Kimberly. *The Body Finder* (The Body Finder Novels series). Harper, 2010.

Dowd, Siobhan. *The London Eye Mystery.* David Fickling Books. 2008.

Downham, Jenny. *You Against Me.* David Fickling Books, 2011.

Doyle, Marissa. *Bewitching Season* (Leland Sisters series). Square Fish, 2009.

Dunlap, Susanne. *The Musician's Daughter.* Bloomsbury, 2008.

Elliott, Patricia. *The Pale Assassin.* Holiday House, 2009.

Evans, Richard Paul. *Michael Vey: The Prisoner of Cell 25* (Michael Vey series). Mercury Ink/Simon Pulse, 2011.

Feinstein, John. *Last Shot* (Final Four Mystery series). Knopf, 2005.

Ferguson, Alane. *The Christopher Killer* (Forensic Mysteries series). Perfection Learning, 2008.

Ferraiolo, Jack D. *The Big Splash.* (Big Splash series). Amulet Books, 2011.

Ferraris, Zoe. *Finding Nouf* (A Katya Hijazi and Nayir al-Sharqi Novel). Houghton Mifflin, 2008. (Adult Series for Teens)

Fforde, Jasper. *The Eyre Affair* (Thursday Next Novels). Viking, 2002. (Adult Series for Teens)

Ford, John C. *The Morgue and Me.* Viking, 2009.

Ford, Michael. *The Poisoned House.* Albert Whitman, 2011.

Fredericks, Mariah. *Crunch Time.* Atheneum Books for Young Readers, 2007.

Fusili, Jim. *Marley Z and the Bloodstained Violin.* Dutton, 2008.

Gerber, Linda. *The Death by Bikini Mysteries* (The Death by . . . Mysteries series). Speak (Penguin), 2011.

Gier, Kerstin. *Ruby Red* (Ruby Red series). Henry Holt, 2011.

Giles, Gail. *What Happened to Cass McBride?* Little, Brown, 2007.

Godwin, Jane. *Falling from Grace.* Holiday House, 2007.

Grabenstein, Chris. *The Crossroads* (Haunted Mystery series). Yearling Books, 2008.

Green, John. *Paper Towns.* Dutton, 2008.

Greenland, Shannon. *Model Spy* (The Specialists series). Puffin, 2007.

Griffin, Adele, and Lisa Brown. *Picture the Dead.* Sourcebooks Fire, 2010.

Grisham, John. *Theodore Boone: Kid Lawyer* (Theodore Boone series). Puffin, 2011.

Haddix, Margaret Peterson. *FOUND* (The Missing series). Simon and Schuster, 2009.

Hahn, Mary Downing. *Mister Death's Blue-Eyed Girls.* Clarion, 2012.

Haines, Kathryn Miller. *The Girl Is Murder.* (The Iris Anderson series). Roaring Brook Press, 2011.

Hamilton, Steve. *The Lock Artist.* Minotaur Books, 2010. (Adult Title for Teens)

Harazin, S. A. *Blood Brothers.* Delacorte, 2007.

Harrington, Kim. *Clarity* (Clarity Novels series). Point, 2011.

Hautman, Pete, and Mary Logue. *Snatched* (Bloodwater series). Putnam Juvenile, 2006.

Healey, Karen. *The Shattering.* Little, Brown, 2011.

Henderson, J. A. *Bunker 10.* Harcourt, 2007.

Henderson, Lauren. *Kiss Me Kill Me* (Scarlett Wakefield series). Delacorte, 2008.

Henry, April. *Girl, Stolen.* Henry Holt, 2010.

———. *The Night She Disappeared.* Henry Holt, 2012.

Higson, Charlie. *SilverFin: A James Bond Adventure* (Young Bond series). Ian Fleming Publications/Hyperion, 2005.

Hodkin, Michelle. *The Unbecoming of Mara Dyer* (The Mara Dyer Trilogy). Simon and Schuster, 2011.

Hoffman, Mary. *The Falconer's Knot: A Story of Friars, Flirtation and Foul Play.* Bloomsbury, 2007.

Horowitz, Anthony. *House of Silk: A Sherlock Holmes Novel* (Sherlock Holmes series). Mulholland Books, 2011. (Adult Series for Teens)

———. *Stormbreaker* (Alex Rider series). Philomel, 2001.

Hyzy, Julie. *State of the Onion* (White House Chef Mysteries series). Berkley, 2008. (Adult Series for Teens)

Janeczko, Paul. *The Dark Game: True Spy Stories.* Candlewick, 2010.

Jinks, Catherine. *Evil Genius* (The Evil Genius series). Harcourt, 2007.

———. *The Reformed Vampire Support Group.* Harcourt, 2009.

Johnson, Maureen. *The Name of the Star* (The Shades of London series). Putnam, 2011.

Johnston, Jeffry. *Fragments.* Simon Pulse, 2007.

Jones, Patrick. *Cheated.* Walker, 2008.

Juby, Susan. *Getting the Girl: A Guide to Private Investigation, Surveillance and Cookery.* HarperTeen, 2008.

King, A. S. *Please Ignore Vera Dietz.* Knopf, 2010.

Lane, Andrew. *Death Cloud* (Sherlock Holmes: The Legend Begins series). Farrar, Straus and Giroux, 2010.

Larbalestier, Justine. *Liar.* Bloomsbury, 2009.

Laurie, Victoria. *Abby Cooper, Psychic Eye* (Psychic Eye Mysteries series). Signet, 2004. (Adult Series for Teens)

Layman, John, and Rob Guillory. *Chew: Volume 1, Taster's Choice* (Chew series). Image Comics, 2009.

Leck, James. *The Adventures of Jack Lime.* Kids Can Press, 2010.

Lee, Y. S. *The Agency: A Spy in the House* (A Mary Quinn Mystery). Candlewick, 2009.

Low, Dene. *Petronella Saves Nearly Everyone: The Entomological Tales of Augustus T. Percival.* Houghton Mifflin, 2009.

Ludwig, Elisa. *Pretty Crooked* (Pretty Crooked Trilogy). HarperCollins, 2012.

Lupton, Rosamund. *Sister: A Novel.* Broadway, 2011. (Adult Title for Teens)

Lynch, Chris. *Kill Switch.* Simon and Schuster, 2012.

MacCready, Robin Merrow. *Buried.* Dutton Juvenile, 2006.

Mackall, Dandi Daley. *The Silence of Murder.* Knopf, 2011.

MacLean, Sarah. *The Season.* Orchard Books, 2009.

Maguire, Eden. *Beautiful Dead: Jonas* (Beautiful Dead series). Sourcebooks Fire, 2010.

Mason, Sarah. *Playing James.* Ballantine Books, 2004. (Adult Title for Teens)

McCleary, Carol. *The Alchemy of Murder* (Murder series). Forge, 2010. (Adult Series for Teens)

McClintock, Norah. *Dooley Takes the Fall* (Ryan Dooley Mysteries). Red Deer Press, 2008.

McGowan, Anthony. *The Knife That Killed Me.* Delacorte, 2010.

McMann, Lisa. *Cryer's Cross.* Simon Pulse, 2011.

———. *Dead to You.* Simon Pulse, 2012.

———. *Wake* (Wake Trilogy). Simon Pulse, 2008.

Meldrum, Christina. *Madapple.* Knopf, 2008.

Miller, Barnabas, and Jordan Orlando. *7 Souls.* Random House Children's Books, 2010.

Mitchell, Saundra. *Shadowed Summer.* Delacorte, 2009.

Moriarty, Jaclyn. *The Murder of Bindy MacKenzie.* Arthur A. Levine Books, 2006.

Neri, G., and Randy DuBurke. *Yummy: The Last Days of a Southside Shorty.* Lee and Low, 2010.

Nixon, Joan Lowery. *The Other Side of Dark.* Delacorte (Reprint), 2011.

Northrup, Michael. *Gentlemen.* Scholastic, 2009.

Olsen, Greg. *Envy* (Empty Coffin series). Splinter, 2011.

Parker, Robert. *The Boxer and the Spy*. Philomel, 2008.
———. *Chasing the Bear: A Young Spenser Novel*. Philomel, 2009.
Patterson, James. *The Angel Experiment* (Maximum Ride series). Little, Brown, 2005.
Pauley, Kimberly. *Cat Girl's Day Off*. Tu Books (Lee and Low), 2012.
Peacock, Kathleen. *Hemlock* (Hemlock series). HarperCollins, 2012.
Pearson, Mary. *The Adoration of Jenna Fox* (The Jenna Fox Chronicles series). Henry Holt, 2008.
Perez, Marlene. *Dead Is the New Black* (Dead Is series). Graphia, 2008.
Pfeffer, Susan Beth. *Blood Wounds*. Harcourt Children's Books, 2011.
Plum-Ucci, Carol. *Following Christopher Creed*. Harcourt, 2011.
———. *The Night My Sister Went Missing*. Harcourt, 2008.
Poznanski, Ursula. *Erebos*. Annick Press, 2010.
Price, Charlie. *Dead Connection*. Roaring Brook Press, 2006.
———. *Desert Angel*. Farrar, Straus and Giroux, 2011.
———. *The Interrogation of Gabriel James*. Farrar, Straus and Giroux, 2010.
Reich, Christopher. (Adult Author for Teens)
Reichs, Kathy. *Virals* (Virals series). Razorbill, 2010.
Reid, Kimberly. *My Own Worst Frenemy* (Langdon Prep series). Dafina, 2011.
Reiss, Kathryn. *Blackthorn Winter*. Harcourt, 2006.
Renn, Diana. *Tokyo Heist*. Viking, 2012.
Riggs, Ransom. *Miss Peregrine's Home for Peculiar Children*. Quirk Books, 2011.
Rosenfield, Kat. *Amelia Anne Is Dead and Gone*. Dutton, 2012.
Roth, Veronica. *Divergent* (Divergent series). Katharine Tegen Books, 2012.
Runholt, Susan. *The Mystery of the Third Lucretia* (Kari + Lucas Mystery series). Puffin, 2009.
Scheier, Leah. *Secret Letters*. Hyperion, 2012.
Schrefer, Eliot. *The Deadly Sister*. Scholastic, 2010.
Sedgwick, Marcus. *Revolver*. Roaring Brook Press, 2010.
———. *White Crow*. Roaring Brook Press, 2011.
Sheinkin, Steve. *The Notorious Benedict Arnold: A True Story of Adventure, Heroism, and Treachery*. Flash Point/Roaring Brook Press, 2011.
Shepard, Sara. *The Lying Game* (Lying Game series). HarperTeen, 2011.
———. *Pretty Little Liars* (Pretty Little Liars series). HarperTeen, 2006.
Shoemaker, Tim. *Code of Silence* (Code of Silence series). Zondervan, 2012.
Shusterman, Neal. *Unwind* (Unwind Dystology series). Simon and Schuster Books for Young Readers, 2007.
Silvey, Craig. *Jasper Jones*. Knopf, 2009.
Smith, Alexander Gordon. *Lockdown* (Escape from Furnace series). Farrar, Straus and Giroux, 2009.
Springer, Nancy. *The Case of the Missing Marquess* (Enola Holmes Mysteries). Philomel, 2006.

Staub, Wendy Corsi. *Lily Dale Awakening* (Lily Dale series). Walker, 2007.

Stolarz, Laurie Faria. *Project 17.* Hyperion, 2007.

Strasser, Todd. *Kill You Last* (The Thrillogy series). Egmont, 2011.

Stratton, Allan. *Borderline.* HarperCollins, 2010.

Suma, Nova Ren. *Imaginary Girls.* Dutton, 2011.

Summer, Courtney. *Fall for Anything.* St. Martin's Griffin, 2010.

Taylor, Brooke. *Undone.* Walker, 2008.

Taylor, Laini. *Daughter of Smoke and Bone* (Daughter of Smoke and Bone series). Little, Brown, 2011.

Tullson, Diane. *Riley Park.* Orca Soundings, 2009.

Valentine, Jenny. *Me, the Missing and the Dead.* HarperTeen, 2008.

Ward, Rachel. *Numbers* (Numbers series). Chicken House, 2010.

Warman, Jessica. *Between.* Walker, 2011.

Weingarten, Lynn. *Wherever Nina Lies.* Point (Scholastic), 2009.

Welsh, T. K. *Resurrection Men.* Dutton, 2007.

Weston, Robert Paul. *Dust City.* Razorbill, 2010.

Wilson, F. Paul. *Jack: Secret Histories* (Young Repairman Jack series). Tor Teen, 2009.

Winspear, Jacqueline. *Maisie Dobbs* (Maisie Dobbs Mysteries). Penguin, 2004. (Adult Series for Teens)

Wooding, Chris. *Malice* (Malice series). Scholastic, 2010.

Wynne-Jones, Tim. *Blink and Caution.* Candlewick, 2011.

Yancey, Rick. *The Monstrumologist* (The Monstrumologist series). Simon and Schuster Books for Young Readers, 2010.

MYSTERIES IN GRAPHIC AND ILLUSTRATED NOVEL FORMATS

Barton, Chris. *Can I See Your ID? True Stories of False Identities.* Dial, 2011. Nonfiction and True Crime.

Campbell, Eddie. *The Black Diamond Detective Agency.* First Second, 2007. Mysteries in Time and Place—Historical Mysteries.

Griffin, Adele, and Lisa Brown. *Picture the Dead.* Sourcebooks Fire, 2010. Mysteries in Time and Place—Historical Mysteries.

Layman, John, and Rob Guillory. *Chew: Volume 1, Taster's Choice* (Chew series). Image Comics, 2009. Fantastic and Paranormal Mysteries—Supersleuths and Special Powers.

Neri, G., and Randy DuBurke. *Yummy: The Last Days of a Southside Shorty.* Lee and Low, 2010. Realistic Mysteries—Undaunted Detectives.

Wooding, Chris. *Malice* (Malice series). Scholastic, 2010. Fantastic and Paranormal Mysteries—Dark Forces.

INDEX